Conservative Republican Myths

How They Try to Trick Each Other, and Us Patriots, too!

by

Joseph Zodl

B.A., Political Science, Fordham University
M.A., Political Science, The New School for Social Research
M.B.A., International Business, Western International University

Copyright 2021 by Joseph Zodl

Other books by Joseph Zodl:

Export-Import: Everything You and Your Company Need to Know to Compete in World Markets

Our Fascinating Presidents: Delectable Morsels of Presidential Trivia

The President's Son Was Kidnapped!

Reverend Brother John and Other Stories

The Republic: Book XI (Book 11)

Table of Contents

Introduction

Once there was a Conservative Senator who would not eat in the Senate restaurant because they served liberal portions. He would not shop at the dollar discount store because they gave liberal discounts. He no longer speaks to his sister who moved to Liberal, Kansas.

Once there was a Liberal Senator who would not wear conservative three-piece suits. He would not invest in money market certificates because they were conservative investments. Al Gore is no longer speaking to him because he refuses to drive conservatively.

So we can quickly see the words can mean different things. What do we mean in application to political matters? The liberals say they are progressive and the conservatives are not. The liberals say government can properly address many problems and the conservatives say not. The conservatives say that individuals should have as much personal freedom as possible, and that when problems are addressed by government, it should be at the lowest possible level: city rather than state, state rather than federal.

Yet on abortion, the liberals say that individuals should have the right to choose. Many are inherently against abortions, though, and support local centers which provide free maternity care and adoption referral, as I do. The conservatives say it should be up to the government which should outlaw abortions.[1]

All very confusing! We live in a confusing era, and much of this confusion seems to be generated by the myths of the Conservative Republicans. (Are there any other kind today? Many will say "no, and we're proud of it.")

Some Conservatives will undoubtedly complain that this little book does not offer any solutions to the many problems it discusses. Yes, thank you for noticing. The focus here bring up myths, point out that they are myths, and support those points with proof: facts and logic. So the Conservative Myths are the focus of the discussion at hand.

Let's take a close look at some of the myths.

---

[1] See the chapter, "Abortions" for development of this issue.

Socialism and Capitalism

Myths:

"Socialism has no place in the U.S. economy."

"We don't want to live under socialism."

"Business is the backbone of the United States and its economy."

The U.S. Economy

Some Conservative Republicans say, "the United States has the greatest economy in the world" and I will agree. Some Conservative Republicans say, "and the United States has the greatest economy in the history of the world" and I will agree. Then some Conservative Republicans say, "and I don't want any socialism in the United States" whereby they contradict their first two statements.

What is Socialism?

Most Conservative Republicans don't have a good working definition of socialism. Here is one we can use: "Socialism is the government ownership of the means of production and/or distribution of goods and/or services."

So that is a lot to say. First, we are including "goods and services" together, which most economists do to describe what an economy produces, exports, imports, and consumes. Production can be growing corn in the field, computer software, or airline service. Distribution is how it gets to the consumer.[2] Some goods and services are

---

[2] When we say "consumer" we generally mean the individual purchasing the corn, software, or airline

exports, produced in the U.S. but not consumed here (corn that is exported, an airline ticket on a U.S. airline bought by a foreign person). Some are imports, produced elsewhere but consumed here (electronics that are imported, an airline ticket on a foreign airline bought by a U.S. person).[3]

Living Under Socialism Can't Happen

Since socialism is an economic system in which the government takes ownership, but not a governing system, it is impossible to live under socialism. A country's economic life can exist as an economic system. A country may live under a democratic government but have a socialist economy. Another may live under an autocratic government but have an autocratic government.

So Conservative Republicans are frightened of something that can't happen, which makes zero sense. They would be better off sitting around being frightened of a meteor screaming down from the sky and crushing them and pounding what's left into the ground (which could happen, while unlikely).

The U.S. Mixed Economy

---

service. But we also say "consumers are responsible for about 70% of the United States Gross Domestic Product ("USGDP"). What about the rest? Government and business consume goods and services in the course of the activities that are never supplied to consumers. Bullets for basic training and photocopies in the office are examples. So too are airline tickets to move personnel around. These are the costs of operations. Business will ultimately have something to sell (although they are not selling their photocopies), and government as well as there are some service fees for some government services, such as admission to national parks.

[3] For clarity on the airline tickets: a foreign person (in Japan) buys a ticket on United Airlines to come to the United States and return. That is counted as an export of U.S. services by United Airlines to Japan. A U.S. person buys a ticket on Japan Airlines to go to Japan and return. That is counted as an import of Japanese Services by Japan Airlines to the United States.

Our economy is largely based on capitalism. Were we to have no socialism, our entire economy would be capitalism. What would that look like?

First, all public libraries would have to shut down immediately. They are government ownership of a means of production of services (we classify them as providing a service, because the lend, but do not sell books, although some socialist libraries do run capitalist used book sales from time to time as fundraisers).

Our public libraries, then, buy books from capitalist book publishers, lend them out free of charge[4] in competition with capitalist booksellers. In some cases, someone does not buy a book that they would have otherwise, because they can get it free of charge for a long enough period of time to read it. I have a personal library, but rarely buy a book these days unless it is a nonfiction book that I want to be able to easily refer back to.

Students who need a book for research don't have to buy every book for every aspect research of every paper. In fact, let's look at that more closely. Suppose you and I are taking an American History class and our assignment is to compare the Articles of Confederation and the Constitution. We have no public libraries anymore, thanks to the Conservative Republicans. I buy a book on the Articles of Confederation and you buy one on the Constitution. After we each finish our necessary research in our book, we trade books. We bring in more students until we have the entire class of 20. Now we have a library of 20 books for us to use. And so we reinvent the natural concept of a

---

[4] Not free of cost, as everything is a cost, but the cost is borne by taxpayers for the benefit of all in the community who wish to use the library.

lending library. Make it a government owned entity to benefit the entire community and we have socialism.

North Dakota is a Conservative Republican state and has an unusual form of socialism and that is the Bank of North Dakota. This is a state-owned and state-managed where all state funds are deposited, and all checks written from those deposits. But local governments and any individual (must be a resident of North Dakota) may open an account as well. The Bank of North Dakota is an interesting institution (https://bnd.nd.gov/public/). It competes with capitalist banks operating within North Dakota,[5] and simultaneously generates profits that are turned over to the state treasury. So the North Dakotans pay just a little bit less in state taxes each year.

Would the national Conservative Republicans want to shut down the Bank? They say they don't want any socialism, but there it is. Would they pass federal legislation to forbid socialism in the banking system? But then they also say that decisions should be made at the lowest level, that states should run their own affairs as much as possible without interference from the federal government. Alas! They are in a corner they built themselves.

Utah is a Conservative Republican state and they love their socialist liquor stores. Alcohol is sold in bars and restaurants, and grocery stores and convenience stores sell beer as well. But beer above 5% ABV ("alcohol by volume"), wine, and hard liquor are

---

[5] Although competition is limited by law, because of the state government being required (by North Dakota's law) to use only the Bank of North Dakota. So commercial financial institutions cannot compete for the state's financial business.

only available through state owned liquor stores. (This does create competition on some beers between capitalism and socialism, but it seems to be working out.) The socialist liquor stores sell liquor at a profit, and that money goes into the state treasury. So that is just a little bit less Utahans pay in taxes, and they love it.

Would the national Conservative Republicans shut down these socialist liquor stores. Or would they allow a state to run its own affairs? There are again in their self-built corner, but here they would have to amend the Constitution, as the decision by Utah to have socialist liquor stores is protected by the Constitution as a specific state's right.[6]

Would you like to really confront and confuse a Conservative Republican? Here we have Medicare which is a socialist system (insurance system owned and managed by the federal government). In recent years, Medicare Part C has come about. This is an option where Medicare recipients can choose to have a plan that is delivered via a commercial insurance carrier, such as Blue Cross/Blue Shield, Humana, United, etc. It all gets very complicated, and if you are not on Medicare, you have undoubtedly seen the television advertising flood by insurance carriers towards the end of each calendar year. This is because from October 15 and December 7 each year, Medicare enrollees can switch among the various choices. If you are on Medicare, you are also getting a flood of mail each year. So this is socialism supporting capitalistic insurance carriers at the same time that the socialist system (original Medicare) is competing alongside them.

---

[6] The 21st Amendment, Section 2.

But wait! While Medicare Advantage generally covers prescription drugs purchased through physical pharmacies, most of the commercial insurance carriers have their online pharmacies also. In many cases, there is an identical copay for drugs purchased either way. In some cases, the drugs have zero copay when ordered through the online pharmacy. So, the capitalist insurance carrier that is supported by a socialist insurance system is competing with its client capitalist pharmacies and sometimes undercutting them. For drugs that are taken regularly, the insurance carrier's online pharmacy is generally a better deal. Free is better than copay, and delivery is free as well. For something like an antibiotic, for someone who needs to start taking it today, the physical pharmacy around the corner is still a better deal.

So we have socialism supporting capitalism at the same time it competes with capitalism, and also providing a capitalistic enterprise with control over a distribution network that allows it to compete against its own clients. Everyone seems to have plenty of choices that are working for them, so let's cheer it on!

Professional football stadiums tend to be socialist. If an expansion team is being considered, the investors usually do not pick a city until there is a guarantee is in front of them that a socialist stadium will be built.

The investors aren't investing in a football team because they like to watch football. They can do that anyway. These investors tend to be on a scale where they can fly to any city in a private jet to watch the game from a skybox. They are investing to maximize the owners' wealth.[7] Football teams can be very profitable and very helpful in maximizing the owners' wealth.

What about the stadiums, then? Why wouldn't the investors want to maximize their wealth by owning the stadiums as well? There are parking fees, rent paid by concessionaires, and on and on. The reason is that the stadium isn't where the profits are. That is where the losses are. The profits are in the team.

Suppose we hear a football expansion team is thinking of opening up in a particular city. Someone suggests we build the stadium ourselves and make the easy money. But a professional football team plays 16 games over a 17-week period, not counting exhibition games and the Super Bowl. Half the games are away games. So if we build the stadium ourselves we have occupancy for eight days out of the year, and 357 vacancy days in a non-leap year (358 vacancy days in a leap year). We have to pay off the a mortgage for (likely) hundreds of millions of dollars for the cost of land and the building and insurance. We'll need security guards and cameras on vacant days as well as occupancy days, lest someone come along and take the computers, furniture, and copper tubing. So we have a year's worth of expenses and eight days' worth of income.

Can we raise our price enough to break even? The investors of the team won't want to hear that. If we discuss prices that are high enough to break even, and cut seriously into their profits, they are likely to pick another city.

---

[7] See "Jobs, Jobs, Jobs."

Can we find tenants for the other days, such as concerts and auto shows? Likely they already have a site for each year. To try to get the business away from them, we will have to make them a better offer than they have now. That means providing more at a lower cost (increasing our costs and lowering our income compared to the competition). We may end up in a price war, but end up getting some of these temporary tenants. We can also compete for new events coming into town. Possibly in a few years we will get close to breaking even, but will we ever show a profit?

So here the logical answer is for a socialist stadium, losing money and being supported by the taxpayers, supporting a capitalist football team that is making money (maximizing the owners' wealth) or if won't happen.

Some people will argue, "but the professional football team creates jobs and that is worth the taxpayers' subsidizing." But see "Jobs, Jobs, Jobs" for the argument against this. That doesn't mean that a socialist stadium and capitalist team aren't the right way to go (they seem the only way to go), but it is always worth looking at the reality of how things are.

Clearly, then, we have not a capitalist economy, and we will never live under socialism, but have a mixed economy of capitalism and socialism. Sometimes socialism functions where capitalism won't, sometimes it supports capitalism, sometimes it competes with capitalism. Sometimes (Utah) it just replaces what could otherwise be capitalism.

Fire Departments

Fire departments? Yes, very relevant. In colonial America, some fire brigades were formed in communities as capitalist organizations following the insurance model. The insurance model is that you pay premiums for fire insurance to a company that is accepting that risk, and pays the claim if you have a fire. **That** insurance company, not some other one down the street.

So if you wanted fire **protection** from one of the community fire brigades, you paid them a fee, and generally received a plaque to put by your front door. If there was a fire, the brigade you paid would attempt to put out the fire, with bucket brigades (hence the name "brigades") and other means available at the time. The other brigades would do nothing. If you paid no brigade, then no brigade would respond. Compare to: if you a policy and pay a premium to Insurance Company A, it is up to them to pay a claim, not Insurance Company B. If you do not pay for fire insurance from any insurance company, then no insurance company will pay your claim. That is the capitalistic model. Some fire brigades were out to make a profit, although some were designed to be nonprofit (to cover their expenses with the homeowner's fees, thus breaking even) but still working the same way.

This didn't work so well in terms of someone who didn't pay anyone a fee, or whose fire brigade was busy on the other side of town, with a fire spreading quickly in a neighborhood of wooden buildings.

Eventually, fire departments became owned and operated by local governments, supported by everyone's taxes, and available to anyone who had a fire. So this was a move to the socialist model. Many of the most conservative Americans today do not realize this, and say that "it isn't capitalism or socialism; it is an essential government service." That's because the moves over time have brought it to be seen as an essential government service. But go down the street and point out to your conservative friends a firehouse that has a sign, "Hook & Ladder **Company** No. 1." That is a nod to the early days when the fire brigades were for-profit, capitalistic companies, which is a distant part of firefighters' heritage.

"Business is the backbone of the United States and its economy."
I hold that "We the People" are the backbone of both. We have lots of people who are involved in the business world and lots of people who aren't: the members of the military, public school teachers, and employees of nonprofit organizations, to name a few, all of whom do important work for the country. We would sorely miss any one group. But these are people, not institutions as such. And then there is the next generation coming along, who are still full-time students, preparing for the futures. Yes, all of the people in the groups I mentioned **interface** with business; an elementary school child can buy a candy bar from a business enterprise, which was bought from a candy manufacturer, who bought chocolate, sugar, milk, wrappers, and other components from other businesses. But that proves that business needs the consumers (people) and that demand drives the economy. Business does not drive the economy because it only responds to demand and anticipated demand.

Creating Money, The Budget, The Deficit, and The Debt

Myths:

"The Democrats just want to print money and then print more, which will bankrupt the country."

"All the Democrats want to do is tax and spend.'

"The debt is all the Democrats' fault."

"Reagan proved deficits don't matter" (Dick Cheney).

Printing Money

Printing money has noting do to with government spending. Repeat. Printing money has nothing to do with government spending.

Proof: When you received your $1,200 payment under the 2020 CARES Act, did the mail show up with an envelope of twelve $100 bills from the U.S. Treasury? Or 60 $20 bills? No? It was either by check or direct deposit. usually via the ACH (Automated Clearinghouse system).

Further Proof: If the U.S. Department of Defense buys new fighter jets, do they set an armored truck full of cash to the manufacturer, with a driver and a pilot, where they unload the cash, and then the pilot flies the plane back to base while the driver goes back for another pilot and truckload full of cash? No, the money is transferred by direct deposit and a pilot flies the plane to base.

What is money in the first place? The classical definition, generally accepted is that money is:

A) A measure of value.

B) A unit of exchange that has a value.

C) A method of storage and investment, as well as selling and buying.

If something is generally accepted as meeting these three standards, it is generally accepted as money. Something can be accepted as meeting these three standards but only by even as few as two parties. This is where two parties meet and barter: my desk for your refrigerator. It doesn't have to be accepted by anyone else because the transaction doesn't affect anyone else. Here we say "the objects of the barter are **acting as money**."

But then what is cash? Currency and coins, of course. But sometimes someone says, "I am paying cash for a new car" but what they really mean is that they have money in the bank and will bring a cashier's check for the correct amount to the car dealer. Further, we have checks, money orders, and so on, as well as debit cards. Credit cards are often used for routine expenses by those who pay the bill by the end of the month (paying no interest on what is really a short-term loan) but these are still credit transactions.

By currency, we generally mean printed money, but most people also think of it as printed money plus coins. But then there are foreign exchange traders who trade electronically, and no currency as defined here changes hands, but they say, "I trade foreign currencies."

There is a lot of confusion. Let's slice through it as fast as possible.

The federal government prints money, but not to pay its bills; it is to give fluidity to the economy by sending it through the banking system.[8] More later. It obtains money to spend via taxes and fees ("fees" is to include income to the federal government that is other than taxes, such an entry fee for a national park), or borrowing. That's it.

The United States has an approximate Growth Domestic Product of $20 trillion ($20,000,000,000). How much is that? This is a good time to develop this perspective:

- If you spent a dollar per second for 12 days, you would spend about $1,000,000 total.

- If you kept it up for 34 years, you would spend about $1,000,000,000 total.

- If you kept it up for 34,000 years, you would spend about $1,000,000,000,000 total.

So $20 trillion is a lot of money!

We also have money that is not involved in buying or selling at the moment. JP Morgan Chase Bank has $1,904,203,000,000 in deposits[9] and the other largest banks are well over a trillion dollars, too.

---

[8] The U.S. Mint https://www.usmint.gov/ and U.S. Bureau of Engraving and Printing https://www.moneyfactory.gov/ have much interesting information available on their websites, and free tours are available, too.
[9] https://www.mx.com/moneysummit/biggest-us-banks-by-deposits is as good a resource as any readily available.

So there is a lot of money out there! Could it all be covered by coins and currency? Total U.S. coins minted and currency printed by the U.S. Treasury that are outstanding as of September 30, 2020[10] are:

Currency in Circulation	$2,133,477,052,438
Coins in Circulation	$ 49,898,794,332
Total in Circulation	$2,183,375,846,770

So a good deal of money consists of electronic entries. What is the place of coins and currency? They are more and more petty cash in a modern economy because so much money is electronic. We get our paycheck direct-deposited, we designate a payment for a mortgage that is sent directly, so money, as we defined it, changed hands, but no currency or coins changed hands. So the need for currency and coins in our huge modern economy is really not so great.

This, in itself, makes an argument against those conservatives (not all!) who advise going back to the gold standard. There is just too much money floating around, including printed money, coins, and electronic money, for gold to effectively back it without causing massive inflation and slowing the economy. That's a long discussion it itself so I will leave the interested reader to other published materials on the subject.

---

[10] https://www.fiscal.treasury.gov/reports-statements/treasury-bulletin/

How do currency and coins circulate in the economy? Your paycheck is directed deposited from your employer's bank account to yours. You go to the bank, or the ATM, and withdraw $20.00 for a cash expense. Let's say you will put $20.00 in the collection at your religious institution of choice. They take the $20.00 and take it to their bank and deposit it into the account where an electronic entry is made to their account. The $20.00 bill sits in the vault until someone needs petty cash again. So the amount of currency and coins is far less than it was in earlier times.

So, does the government print money to meet its expenses? No, we covered that earlier. Does the Federal Reserve Bank (FRB) print money? No, because that power is in the U.S. government, but we're getting close. The doesn't print any money but **creates** money on its books simply by saying so. ("Banking and Finance," or sometimes called "Money and Capital" is a full semester college course, so trust me on this one.)

One methodology is that the FRB creates money[11] which is then available to the member commercial banks[12] in the FRB role as "lender of last resort" but this is not a common, everyday occurrence. More common is that it buys U.S. government bonds on the open market, thus taking money that it has created for its account and sending it out to pay for the bonds. "Open market" means that the U.S. Treasury has already issued the bond, perhaps even years ago, and it is available for purchase from a private party

---

[11] In the time frame between the Second Bank of the United States and the Federal Reserve Bank, commercial banks created the money (they still do in terms of fractional reserve banking) which in earlier times meant printing their own currency. Visit a coin and currency dealer and you'll probably be able to see some. If you visit New York, I always recommend a stop at the Museum of American Finance (https://www.moaf.org/) which has lots of currency and coins in their collection.
[12] The commercial member banks own the Federal Reserve Bank, not the federal government. See, I said banking and finance is complicated.

(often commercial banks) on the open market.[13] So the private party gets an electronic transfer originating from the FRB and new money enters the economy. This is done if the FRB wants to speed up the economy, but it can be inflationary (more customers with more money chasing the limited available supply of goods convinces sellers it's time to raise prices). The FRB can sell bonds on the marketplace, bring in money from their customer, place it on their books, and then erase the money from their books. This is done when the FRB wants to slow an economy that is moving too rapidly, and causing too much inflation.[14] All of this is done without coins or currency. So printing money has nothing to do with how money is created and uncreated in a modern economy; we just enough to take care of petty cash needs without a shortage of physical printed currency and minted coins.

To sum up then: money is created by the banking system, and, in the U.S., when we refer to that action, we generally mean by the Federal Reserve Bank, as with central banks in other countries with advanced economies. Coins and currency are created by the U.S. government, and are sold to the Federal Reserve Bank, but only enter the economy when the FRB sells them to commercial banks to take care of the petty cash needs of the economy.

The federal government, on the other hand, collects money through taxes and fees, and borrows money through sales of securities[15] and spends it according to appropriations by Congress.[16]

---

[13] Start here https://www.nyse.com/markets/bonds and research as deeply as you want.
[14] I said it was complicated.
[15] We've referred to these as bonds. Actually, there are three basic forms: bills, for one year or less, notes

Tax and Spend

This argument was made very forcefully against Clinton during the 1992 campaign. But was this factual, that this is "all" he wanted to do? No, he wanted to get America back on its feet and make America strong again. Reagan and George H. W. Bush had quadrupled the national debt, through fiscal conservative deficit spending, in only 12 years.[17] Clinton balanced the budget and even put us into surplus using fiscal liberal balanced budget policies as of 1998. So by 1998, as some bonds from 1968 came due, as for example, bonds financing the Vietnam War at the time, were paid off with the surplus.[18]

This lasted through September 30, 2001, when George W. Bush's first budget went into effect, and we were back in deficit again. So by 2002 we are no longer paying off the Vietnam War debt. As those 30 year bonds came due, the Bush administration borrowed more money to pay off the creditors. If we take the end of the Vietnam War as 1975, then the last Vietnam War debt came due in 2005. Because Bush renewed the debt, we will continue paying interest on the Vietnam War up to at least 2035.

George W. Bush, following in his father's and Reagan's footsteps as a fiscal conservative, doubled the national debt (he only had eight years), by 2009 and the end of his second term. We all remember the condition he left the country in at the time.

---

for two, three, five, seven, or 10 years, and bonds are for 30 years.
[16] As per Article One, Section Nine, Clause Seven, of the United States Constitution.
[17] Of course we backup our data. That's the liberal way. See
https://www.treasurydirect.gov/govt/reports/pd/histdebt/histdebt.htm
[18] No, the federal government didn't spend the surplus. If it had, it wouldn't have been a surplus.

Obama never brought us to a balanced budget (he did have a Republican Congress during most of his administration), but he did reduce the deficits seven out of eight years and so move us towards a balanced budget once again.[19] Then Donald Trump began to run trillion dollar deficits (this was prior to COVID 19). So that is a clear pattern.

Closing this off, what is, after all, the difference between the deficit and the debt? The deficit is our shortfall each year our debt is what we owe. If the deficit becomes a surplus, then that's what we have left over. Here is an example, admittedly oversimplified:

Consider a household where the income is $50,000 per year and between mortgage, outstanding car loan, and other debts, they owe $300,000. Are they in trouble? We can't tell yet.

A new fact: They pay their bills, including the payments on their debts, and altogether that is $51,000 per year. Yes, they are in trouble. They are spending $1,000 more this year than they take in. So next year their debt is $301,000 and that is not a good direction.

A different fact: They pay their bills, including the payments on their debts, and altogether that is $49,000 per year. No, they are not in trouble. They are $1,000 ahead at the end of the year. So their assets total $1,000 and their debt $300,000, which

---

[19] https://www.govinfo.gov/app/collection/BUDGET/

means their balance sheet says they are net $299,000, paying off the debt and gaining more savings, so they are going in the right direction.[20]

Conservative Deficit Spending

So in the end, it was a myth that all Clinton wanted to do was "tax and spend." He wanted to stop the borrowing and the mounting debt. By balancing the budget, he reduced the drain on available capital by reducing the amount of federal spending. This ended the Bush Recession of 1992 and moved us forward to higher employment, Gross Domestic Product growth, and tremendous growth in the stock market. We can go through other administrations, too, but the Democrats consistently work towards a balanced budget and a stronger America; the Republicans consistently work towards higher debt and a weaker America. I can't say all Democrats achieve a balanced budget; often a Republican Congress stops them.

Rationalization by Republicans: "Reagan proved that deficits don't matter" (Dick Cheney)[21] Well, if you believe that, then you are a fiscal conservative. If you believe deficits do matter, that a balanced budget is better, and a surplus is even better, then you are a fiscal liberal.

So why do the Democrats get the blame for higher national debt? And how, at the same

---

[20] The national debt is often compared to the Gross Domestic Product (GDP) , which are not that much different. Some say, "look, we owe as much as produce each year." Accountants among us will note that the debt is a balance sheet net number and the GDP is an income statement. Further, the debt is the federal government's debt and the GDP is the national economy's production. It is like comparing your income statement to my balance sheet, which have no relationship and therefore the comparison has no relevance. That is not to suggest that the debt isn't high, or that it isn't important. It is high and it is important, and that is why we need more fiscal liberals in charge of the country.
[21] https://www.chicagotribune.com/news/ct-xpm-2004-01-12-0401120168-story.html

time, can the conservatives place blame for "tax and spend" which means living within the budget? The only answer I can come up with is that the Republicans are good at coming up with delusional stories and spreading them as far and wide as they can.

The Laffer Curve seems to be the basis of Cheney's conclusion, however, and of the fiscal conservative policies from Reagan until now. Even Trump (before COVID 19) was skyrocketing the deficit to a trillion dollars a year. In simplified form, Arthur Laffer has concluded that if we lower taxes, we don't have to lower spending to balance the budget. Lower taxes will do this. The conservatives accept this. So they have tax cut after tax cut over the years, and keep increasing spending, so more is constantly going out and less coming in. The Laffer Curve insists that this is the way to balance the budget.

Personally, I believe "tax and spend," spend only what you take in, the fiscal liberal concept, makes more sense. The only way the Laffer Curve can work is if the higher the deficit, the closer you get to a balanced budget, which is ridiculous. President Donald J. Trump did award Arthur Laffer the nation's highest civilian honor, the Presidential Medal of Freedom for "contributions to economic policy." <sigh> I believe Trump really thinks so, as the rest of the fiscal conservatives do.

COVID 19 wreaked havoc on employment on the economy overall, but an examination of the data does show that while unemployment dropped drastically during the Obama Recovery, it leveled off during the Trump Administration before COVID 19.[22] Likewise,

---

[22] https://www.bls.gov/opub/ted/2019/unemployment-rate-unchanged-at-3-point-6-percent-in-may-

we see that the growth of the Gross Domestic Product slowed from 2018 to 2019, before COVID 19.[23] So it appears that the Conservative Republican policies were already beginning to kick in by 2019.

Cut Regulations to Help Business and Help America

Myths:

"There are too many government regulations."

"Business management knows how to run the business better than the government does."

2019.htm#:~:text=In%20May%202019%2C%20the%20unemployment%20rate%20was%20unchanged,April%202019%20and%203.8%20percent%20in%20May%202018.
[23] https://www.bea.gov/data/gdp/gross-domestic-product Go to "Tables Only" which opens an MSOffice Excel file, and then select the worksheet named "Table 5" from the bottom of the page.

"Obama's regulations on business is what strangled the U.S. economy."

How Many Regulations are too Many?

I have not heard a Conservative Republican answer this question. They have to come up with specific numbers even to begin explaining this.

A) The number of regulations is XXX.

B) The correct number of regulations is YYY.

C) Therefore, the excess number of regulations is ZZZ.

Actually, we only need them to tell us any two and we can use basic algebra to solve for the third. But they will not tell. All they do is reach the conclusion that "there are too many" out of thin air.

But is it the number of regulations, or is it specific regulations?

Trump's Executive Order

Donald Trump said that he would eliminate the so-called "job killing regulations" of Obama but if he did so he did not publicize it well. He also did not prove that the regulations killed jobs either, because the prosperity of the Great Obama Recovery gets in the way.

Trump in fact did issue an early executive order that every time a new regulation would be introduced, two would be removed.[24] But that is not a well-thought out directive. Suppose you are Secretary of State and your staff presents you with a proposed new regulation that you feel will improve national security. You are very excited about this! Now you have to direct the staff to find two regulations to repeal. Perhaps they find two regulations that relate to obsolete matters, which now make the regulations obsolete. But that is difficult, because that was pursued already under an Obama Administration initiative. You and your staff can find no regulation that should be eliminated What to do! If your new regulation is important enough for you to prioritize, you have to find two necessary regulations that are a lower priority in national security. So to increase national security by adopting the new regulation you have to reduce national security by eliminating two others. If you feel the one new is more important than the two old, that this what you have to do. But let's give the new regulation a value of 10. The two old ones each have a value of four. So instead of increasing national security by a value of 10, your only way to adopt it is to reduce national security by a value of eight, therefore

---

[24] Actually, it is balancing the incremental costs, so this example is on the regulations themselves *per se* in order to make the principle immediately clear. But you can read the Executive Order for yourself: https://www.whitehouse.gov/presidential-actions/presidential-executive-order-reducing-regulation-controlling-regulatory-costs/

increasing national security by two instead of 10. The Conservative Republicans saw this as a wonderful, wonderful, thing.

So from the Conservative Republican point of view, focusing on the number of regulations being too many (although they will not explain this), rather than the quality of whether a regulation is beneficial or not, by how much, if it is now obsolete, and so on.

Capitalists Hate Competition and Love/Hate Regulations.

Here I bring in individual capitalists rather than capitalism as a whole. First, let's agree that competition is the opposite of monopoly. With anyone who wants to argue, "competition is good; it can lower prices, bring about better products and service, and bring about innovation" I will have no argument. I totally agree, from the point of view of the national economy and the public interest. But it is the **capitalist** who would prefer not to have competition, which then creates monopoly.

Consider a small town of a few hundred people off an interstate ramp. It has three gas stations with convenience stores and small coffee shops attached (because in addition to the residents, people driving along the freeway make their stops), some religious institutions, one hardware store, one grocery store, and so on. This is a small town in a farming area, where the rural residents come for religious services, pickup supplies, and so on. It is the largest community (including gas stations) for many miles in each direction. Got the picture? Good.

Now suppose one capitalist owns each of the three gas stations (with their side ventures). Unless people in the community want to drive many miles, they will buy from one of those stations, as well as people driving through (trucks buying lots of diesel and drivers wanting to fill their coffee thermoses are highly desired customers). We should expect to see some competition. We should see competition on pricing, specials ("free coffee with 10 gallon or more fill-up") and perhaps each is open 24 hours.

Now suppose one capitalist owns all three. There is no local competition and so he can charge what he wants for gasoline and diesel, unless he drives his prices so high it makes more sense to drive on (unless you are almost out of gas in which case you are stuck with the pricing). He does not have to offer specials, and he does not have to keep all three open 24 hours. In fact, he can shut down two and open other businesses and, instead of a monopoly of all three gas stations, set up a monopoly of one.[25]

So for a capitalist, something that helps his venture is good, and something that hurts his venture is bad. (It is the basic psychological principle that the human conditions seeks to gain pleasure and avoid pain.) This brings us to the point that a capitalist does not want to be regulated.

Here again, let's take two capitalists, and for simplicity make it a local situation. The local health code and the health inspector. Neither of our subjects want to bother with either one (such nuisances!). They are running restaurants.

---

[25] Of course, this doesn't mean that someone else, perhaps a large chain, may see the situation and decide to come in and compete, or even start a price war that drives this capitalist out of business and creates a monopoly for themselves.

Capitalist A runs an efficient operation and serves only fresh hamburger meat. He would do this regulations or no regulations because he believes that is the honest and appropriate way to operate the restaurant. When the health inspector comes, she has to drop what she is doing to give the nuisance a guided tour to prove she is complying with the health regulations, which she would be doing anyway.

Capitalist B runs a very efficient operation and part of the efficiency is to mix in hamburger meat that has spoiled with fresh hamburger meat. He is aware of the regulations and sees the health inspector as a pest. He has to run to collect the spoiled meat and throw it in the garbage, give the guided tour, and then have to recover the spoiled meat from the garbage and resume the mixing. (The whole idea, of course, being in the interests of public health, and, as with all laws and regulations, the enforcers don't catch everyone, someday he will not move fast enough and get caught.)

Neither one likes the regulations but for different reasons. If, indeed, we repealed the health regulations, then Capitalist B is going to have a more profitable operation for always because he is cutting his costs in a way Capitalist A will not. In fact, B may be able to lower his prices and still make a higher profit than A, with the result of forcing A out of business.

What about lawsuits? (The Conservative Republicans say there are too many of those, too, but will not show us the math. Well, if enough people get sick and we can trace it back to this restaurant, a defense can be "but we broke no law and violated no regulation. How could we be negligent if we were going buy the book?" This may not save the day, but it is a valid defense.

So we could expect that Capitalist A, after considering all the above, will be in favor of the health regulations and health inspector, because they will eventually, the bad operators (hopefully) will get caught, fined, and possibly shut down. If enough of that happens, it may be a deterrence against others doing the same thing. Put it together: The health regulations and inspector are something Capitalist A will put up with out of necessity (believing in following the law and regulations as well in public health). But also recognize it as indirectly to her own advantage by making it more difficult for unfair and dishonest competitors to survive.

So are the regulations and inspector a bother for Capitalist A? Yes.
Do the regulations and inspector help protect Capitalist A's business against unfair competition? Yes.
Do the regulations and inspector benefit society? Yes.
And the Conservative Republicans do not like this sort of thing at all.

But where do Capitalists really **like** regulation? Oh, that's only if it's someone else. The pharmacy will say, "we can do better without the regulatory burdens, but you should check up on those greedy pharmaceutical manufacturers and wholesalers, because that's where the problems are." Big Pharma says, "we can be much more efficient in supply pharmaceuticals to the American people, but you should take a look at the insurance companies." The insurance companies say, "we need more regulation on the medical doctors because they are overprescribing." And so it goes.

"Don't regulate me. Regulate those I have to deal with. If you tie their hands and leave my hands free, the whole world will be better off."

"Obama's regulations on business is what strangled the U.S. economy."
For this to be true, the economy would have had to shrink during the Obama Administration. The Gross Domestic Product growth would have to have slowed, then fallen, unemployment increase, stock market fall, and so on. So let's dismiss the myth because its historical premise is incorrect. We had terrific growth in GDP, employment, and stock market during the Obama years, once we got past the wreckage left by the George W. Bush Administration. Donald Trump tried to take credit for the last two years of the Obama Recovery, until his policies began to initiate the Trump Recession. We saw EARLY signs in 2019, before COVID as he stepped forward with a Republican Congress to increase the annual deficits to over a trillion dollars.[26]

In fact, if we look at the Big Picture, even prior to Trump: we had Nixon, Ford, Reagan, Bush #41, and Bush #43. Examining the economy, we see eight recessions, three stock market crashes (particularly noting the Great Reagan Crash of 1987). Then we see the Great Republican Meltdown and the Great Republican Financial Crisis (which they

---

[26] See "Creating Money, The Budget, The Deficit, and The Debt."

escalated into the Global Financial Crisis) in confluence with the Great Republican Recession of 2008 (George W. Bush's Second Recession, or Fourth Bush Recession[27]) . So we see definite patterns.

In between, we see Carter, Clinton, and Obama in periods called "recoveries." Even the Republicans will call these periods "recoveries" but will not call them the Carter Recovery, Clinton Recovery, or Obama Recovery. Why would they not? Because this establishes an additional definite pattern which leads to the question: "what is the country recovering from?" Why, Conservative Republican policies, of course.

So in summary, we see economic hard times being during Conservative Republican administrations, and the economic recoveries, back to prosperity, during Liberal Democratic administrations. Over and over and over again.

What, then, do we logically end up as a true statement to counterbalance the Conservative Republican myth? Clearly, "Conservative Republican policies are what strangle the U.S. economy." And because of the size of the U.S. economy, this spills over to harm the world economy, and the United States gets worldwide blame.

---

[27] Counting two recessions per Bush.

But Where Do Regulations Come From? By What Authority?

Let's consider the Internal Revenue Service. Everyone seems to agree that the laws and regulations are complicated and cumbersome, but then everyone seems to be in favor of provisions that help them lower their taxes; they are only against provisions that help someone else but not them. And so this is human nature. "If it helps me, it's fair, justice, and right. But if it doesn't help me, then it's unfair, unjust, and wrong."

First we have the Constitution which, in Article One, Section Eight, Clause One, "The Congress shall have Power To lay and collect Taxes...." So that is the initial authority. Then the income tax is specifically authorized under the Sixteenth Amendment.

Under the Constitution, we have the International Revenue Service laws[28] as passed by Congress. So there is the second link in the chain. Examining 16 USC §6513 (c)[29] we see that the due date is April 15 following the taxable calendar year. But there is not listed a place to send our tax return and payment. Dear me! We are required to do something and not being told how. But this is necessary to know or we can't file. So there is an implicit authority by the IRS laws that the Internal Revenue Service will set this up. So we see in 26 Code of Federal Regulations 1.6091-2 (a)(1) that this will depend on the legal residence of the individual filer. That is the third link in the chain.

So where we file depends on the address shown in the instruction booklet. That is set up procedurally, where there are various Internal Revenue Service Centers which can

---

[28] https://www.law.cornell.edu/uscode/text/26
[29] https://www.law.cornell.edu/uscode/text/26/6513

receive our tax returns and payments, depending on our legal residence. So this is the fourth link in the chain. This isn't established at the regulatory level because this can change from time to time and can be changed more easily at this level (regulations generally require a period of time for public comment). This is the fourth link in the chain.

While we do have provisions today for e-filing, and many individuals take advantage of this, imagine if you were Commissioner of Internal Revenue and were ready to make a change of address when a new IRS Service Center was opened, you would have to through the regulatory process. So some things are changed procedurally without needing to be changed at the regulatory process.

Some Conservative Republicans say the power to issue regulations should be taken away from the "unelected bureaucrats" The IRS Commissioner is nominated by the President subject to Senate confirmation. Would it better if candidates for IRS Commissioner (and FBI Director, National Park Service Director, etc., etc.) all ran for office on a regular basis? How many hundreds of names do we add to the ballot and how well will the average voter know all these candidates and the issues they are running on? But then we would have elected bureaucrats, which is something the Conservative Republicans should not object to. Of course, then we might have a duly elected Conservative Republican President and Congress wanting to go in certain directions and duly elected Liberal Democratic Commissioners and Directors who have decided to go in different directions under their own executive authority. (Have the Conservative Republicans ever thought this through?)

There is another idea that they float from time to time, that the power to make the regulations should be given to Congress. Have they looked at the Code of Federal Regulations lately?[30] And the United States Code?[31] Congress has enough to try to work on versus more than doubling its workload. And should all the details of every federal regulation require an Act of Congress? Should Congress have to take time out from important legislation to consider if the definition of "Advanced in value" should be changed from the current regulatory provisions?[32] Wouldn't this clog up the system from consider important trade treaties and other legislation? And the Conservative Republicans claim they are in favor of efficient government!

But what they miss is because of the links in the chain, Congress can overrule any regulation by removing the authority of the agency to regulate the detail and provide a specific provision in an Act of Congress. The power is still in the elected representatives should the executive branch create a provision that Congress doesn't feel is in the national interest. That is Constitutional checks and balances which has been with us since 1789. (When some has worked for so long, you would think the Conservative Republicans would be impressed by it.)

---

[30] https://www.law.cornell.edu/cfr/text
[31] https://www.law.cornell.edu/uscode/text
[32] https://www.law.cornell.edu/cfr/text/19/11.6

Which Regulations?

Lastly, I linked to the United States Code, or USC (statutes on the law books), and the United States Code of Federal Regulations, or CFR. Conservative Republicans sometimes point to the CFR and say "see! There are 50 volumes that a business has to read and be ready to follow before it can open its doors. That is just too big a burden." <sigh> But not all apply to every business. Some, such as Title Three, apply to the government (in this case, the President) but can affect the entire country, based on the President's actions. But if you are a farmer Title 7 is of importance; if you are a manufacturing executive or union official, Title 29 should have your attention, but not Title 7. If you are starting a trucking company, you should examine Title 49, but if you are starting an interstate water service (cargo, ferry), Title 46 should be on your desk.

Who would be subject to all 50? I can't think of anyone. So far I haven't met a Conservative Republican who can.

Cut Taxes on the Top 1%

Myths:

"We need to cut taxes on the top 1% because they are the ones who create jobs."

"We need to cut taxes on business because then they will create jobs."

"The Democrats have imposed a death tax on Americans."

"Tax cuts stimulate the economy and create more profit and more jobs, and thus bring in more tax revenue even at the lower rate. Therefore, cutting taxes balances the budget."

Job Creation

First, this idea only works if investment capital (supply) creates jobs, but the opposite is true.[33] Yes, investment capital is a necessity but the fact that we have investment capital does not equal job creation.

In fact, capital that is invested may be a liability to the receiver of the capital. Here is a local credit union with $500,000,000 in deposits. Most of that has been loaned out but as a loan is paid off, they are looking for another member to borrow. They need the loan interest coming in to pay out the interest on the deposits as well as pay the expenses of running the credit union (rent, utilities, employees). This is so whether interest rates are low or high. A commercial bank will also have to show a profit, but a credit union is setup as a nonprofit organization.

---

[33] See "Jobs, Jobs, Jobs."

But let's take the credit union as our first example because it is conveniently a small financial institution. We won the lottery and have a prize of $100,000,000. We will ultimately decide how to invest it (possibly we will hear from many relatives we have long forgotten about and many friends we didn't know we had, all with investment ideas, or simply an idea that they should get a share because…well, just "because." But for the moment, we will put in our credit union account. The balance in our account is now $100,001,00 and that is an asset on our personal financial statement. But it is a **liability** to the credit union. Their assets are loans (money due to come in to them, or "accounts receivable") and their liabilities are deposits (money due for them to pay out (interest) or "accounts payable'). Things have been going smoothly for them, and they have been effectively lending out deposits, but now their deposits (and interest **payable**) have just increased 20%. What to do?

The loan officers are going to have to aggressively solicit loan applications from the credit union members, but how successful with this be? They approach one family that has two car loans and asks if they would like a third car loan. They say, "no, we only have two drivers and we only need to cars." The loan officer says, "but the credit union needs to issue more loans to be able to pay out interest on your deposits. Wouldn't you like to take out a third car loan for $30,000 and pay interest for six years on a car that says parked in the garage, to help us out?" No, there isn't the demand, so the supply isn't needed, not at any interest rate.

They approach someone who had a home improvement loan for $50,000 to refinish the kitchen and bathroom and do some landscaping. They ask, "wouldn't you like to borrow another $50,000 with interest?" The homeowner says, "no, I completed all my projects. I don't need to take out a second loan and pay interest on it."

As a major liability, our $100,000,000 deposit is causing serious, serious, problems for our credit union. Will they borrow money to be able to pay our interest? We may be invited to lunch with the president of the credit union who will ask us to take our business somewhere else.

If we take our money to a large bank, such as Chase, Citibank, Bank of America, or Wells Fargo, with billions upon billions upon dollars of loans outstanding (assets) and billions and billions of dollars of deposits (liabilities), they should be able to absorb our deposit and put it to work effectively, because they are playing at an entirely different level. But the principal is still the same: for a financial institution, deposits, are on the liability sides of the balance sheet.[34] For the depositor, deposits are on the asset side.

---

[34] There is also something called "fractional-reserve banking" which is outside the scope of our brief discussion, but there is plenty of good information available at public libraries and on internet sites, but watch your sources! While this has been an effective aspect of banking for hundreds of years, some Conservative Republicans who have just found out about it and don't understand it, have decided it is Unconstitutional. Somehow.

Estate Taxes

Let's discuss others first. How do the poor approach investment and their estates? They have very little to pass on to the next generation to begin with. A high school dropout[35] An apartment dweller may have a used car and some old furniture and a little savings to pass on to the next generation. They were always in survival mode, not in accumulation mode. Many times, they can't afford life insurance (not that they don't want to have it; the money to pay for it isn't there). So the estate may not be enough to cover unpaid copays or deductibles for the final illness. The assets may need to be sold to cover unpaid bills and there may be nothing left for the funeral expenses. There next generation may end up borrowing money to pay for a low-cost funeral, and so the death itself may be a financial burden to the next generation.

How does the middle class approach investment and estates? We have the lower middle class, the central middle class, and upper middle class, which can have very different lives. Various income and asset brackets have been used to try to place people at one or another level of the pyramid, but it's difficult. Cost of living is different in

---

[35] Let's address an educational issue as long as we're here. Some people higher on the economic pyramid truly look down on the poor as "lazy," "why didn't they just finish their education?" "why don't they go back and get a GED and get their degree now?" Let's focus on the dropout. Some people dropout because they are going to work to help support the family, sometimes there are family problems where a teenager drops out of school as soon as it is legally permissible, leaves town, and never talks to the family again. Bad situations, but think back to when you were in high school. Was there someone you knew who struggled through elementary school classes and by freshman year of high school is still reading and writing at a sixth grade level? If we have people in our society who are above average, then we have people who are below average in ability, by whatever potential ability, intellectual, athletic, or anything else we care to measure (not their fault!). Here I speak from own experience, that while I was a good student, I was a terrible athlete in almost every sport I ever tried, no matter how hard I tried. Some of those I went to school with were good at any sport almost as soon as they took it up, but had trouble on the academic side, not for lack of effort. So we do have some people who drop out of high school simply because "this is too hard" and may live a life towards or at the bottom of the pyramid. They may have lowpaying jobs supplements by food stamps all their lives, and then a low Social Security check with little if any savings because they never made a good income in the first place. Let us not look down on them, but lend them a helping hand when we can.

Alabama versus New York. Someone in a city earning $50,000 per year as a single-person household can be living a more expensive lifestyle than someone in the same city earning $100,000 per year with four school age children. But we can say that most people in the middle class do aspire to move up as best they can. There is definitely a squeeze on the middle class, like a squeeze on a toothpaste tube, but pushing the contents (real people) downward, not upward. Of course I blame the Conservative Republicans, for reasons covered in this book as well as many more. So we have to take some liberal measures to correct the downward plunge.

A person in the middle class may have a house to pass along, some savings, something remaining in an IRA or 401(k) or 401(b) fund, a late model car, and so on. Likely there is life insurance to pay for the final expenses, or at least enough cash to cover them. So here the next generation would receive some inheritance.

And the really, really, rich? Now we get into real estate planning and that is another section below.

At this writing, the exemption is $11,700,000 for an individual, and double that for married couples.[36] So below that level, there is no federal estate tax. Zero. It was

---

[36] While there are plenty of complications on inheritance law generally, because the state law affects the value and status of the estate, fundamentally, the married couple exemption applies if both spouses die simultaneously, such as sometimes happens in a tragic car accident. A common situation is if one spouse dies, there is an individual exemption that applies when the estate passes to the other spouse, and it the individual exemption applies again when that spouse dies, in two separate steps. However, there are many complications, including community property states, so this is just meant as an example, definitely not tax or estate planning advice. Everyone should consult an attorney on estate planning and preparation of a will (if you don't have an attorney, contact your local Bar Association for free referrals). This will enable you to state how assets will be distributed, including that special ring you want someone to have, and alternate heirs if an heir predeceases you. And all this is extra important if you have children

$5,450,000 for an individual and double that for couples. What changed? It was the Republican tax bill of 2017.[37] (It will increase every year, keeping pace with inflation.)

What was the justification? "Sniff, sniff. Our eyes are filled with tears over the poor families that are losing their homes to pay the estate tax. We need to increase the exemption to protect all these people from liberal taxes. You liberals really don't care about the poor or you would be for increasing the exemption as well."

I said, "introduce me to someone who has $5,450,000.01 in assets: house, land, bank accounts, retirement funds, everything who therefore has an estate that would be just over the threshold that exists. If they drop dead tonight, one cent of their estate will be subject to taxes. And after you introduce me to the person who has $5,450,000.01 in assets, prove to me that they are poor." At this point, the Conservative Republicans would turn and walk away, usually, telling me, "there's no sense trying to explain things to you. You just don't understand economics." <sigh>

But according to the Conservative Republicans who explained their position to me, the increase in the exemption was solely to protect the poor. Not the rich! Oh, no, not at all. According to them, everyone at every level of income is subject to the exemption (which is true) and so it is fair (which is questionable).

(who will get custody? Will they receive an extra inheritance for support of the extra child in the family if they accept custody? And who is the alternative if that person predeceases you?) All this can avoid very messy situations. But for most Americans, estate tax planning won't be needed.
[37] The individual states have estate taxes also, and the exemptions, as well as the tax rates, very. We'll omit all those scenarios and limit our discussion to the federal estate tax.

The poor, as discussed above, leaving behind minimal estates and perhaps debt, would not leave an estate subject to the estate tax. Taking the new individual threshold, someone who is middle class and leaves behind a paid-off house, cash assets in their retirement fund, and other assets, of $1,000,000 leaves behind an estate that will not be taxed because it is within the exemption. But that leaves $10,700,000 of the exemption unused. Someone else lived a middle class lifestyle owning and operating a small business and sold it to retire, and dies shortly thereafter with a $5,000,000 estate including the proceeds of the sale and all other assets. Yes, they estate will not be taxed either, because it is within the exemption. That leaves $6,700,000 of the exemption unused. But in all three cases, those estates wouldn't have paid estate taxes anyway under the old exemption, so it doesn't affect them at all.

Now we have someone who had an even more successful small business, designing new software, and eventually sold the company to a large software company for $11,000,000. At the time of death, they left behind a total estate of $11,500,000 and so their estate paid no taxes as it is within the exemption, leaving $200,000 of the exemption unused.

Most people in the United States, if they died tonight, would leave behind an estate that wouldn't be subject to estate taxes because the estates will fall within the exemption. But many of those would have fallen within the old exemption anyway. (And remember, in both cases, double for married couples.

So just who does the exemption benefit? Well by my math, it is only those individuals leaving behind an estate worth $11,700,000.01 or more (double that for married couples). But how much tax? Well, the tax rate is zero for the first $10,000 of **taxable** estate so that still leaves all individual estates of $11,710,000 and less tax-free. It does rise as we go along, to an 18% bracket, to a 20% bracket, and so on. Let's assume an estate is at the top tax rate, for $3,000,000 of **taxable** estate. That means an estate of $14,700,00 total ($11,700,000 under the exemption leaving behind $3,000,000 of **taxable** estate).

What is the tax here? There is first a flat tax of $345,800 (that is the accumulated tax on the first $1,000,000, part at 18%, part at 20%, and so on). Then there is a tax of 40% on the excess over $1,000,000. So that means 40% of the additional $2,000,000, or $800,000 on this basis.

So we have:

Total Estate	$14,700,000
Minus Exemption	$11,700,000
Taxable Portion of Estate	$ 3,000,000
Flat tax on first $1,000,000 of Taxable Portion of Estate	$ 345,800
40% tax on excess over $1,000,000 of Taxable Portion of Estate $3,000,000	$ 800,000
Total Tax of $14,700,000 Estate	$ 1,145,800

Effectively, then, that is a tax rate of .779% which we can round up to 8%. An 8% tax rate. Such a deal! If you are an individual, even the first dollar of wages is taxed at 10% and the maximum federal income tax rate is 37%.

What was that about the Conservative Republicans saying this was all about protecting the poor?

Oh, and sometimes they will come up with an argument about how "people in farm country die and leave behind the family farm that is worth millions of dollars and the family has to give it up to pay the estate taxes."

Well, first of all, the family doesn't pay estate taxes. The heirs aren't taxed, the estate is. A tax return is filed by the executor[38] and the taxes come out of an estate.

First, we would have to have a farm valued at more than $11,700,000 for estate taxes to matter. But suppose someone leaves behind a farm valued at $14,700,000? Then the above table applies, with an effective rate of 8%. Someone inherits a farm valued at $14,700,000 and the estate mortgages $1,145,800 of the farm's value to pay the estate taxes. We will weep for Grandma but we still have $14,700,000 worth of assets and $1,145,800 worth of debt, for a net inheritance of $13,554,200. So we still end up with $13,554,200 more than we had before.

―――――――――――――――――――――

[38] Sometimes called an "administrator" or "personal representative" based on state law.

Many farms, and other real estate have mortgages. Suppose the farm is worth
$25,000,000 but there is a mortgage on it that is still a $10,300,000 encumbrance. Why,
then, we a farm that is worth $14,700,000 and the above example applies. We have a
$25,000,000 asset with a total of $11,445,800 worth of debt, which is still $14,700,000
more than we had before (asset minus debt [mortgage] = net value of estate). Most
people would consider this a valuable inheritance.

What is the value of the farm minus the mortgage brings us to $11,700,000? Then we
are once again within the new individual exemption and the estate pays no taxes.

**Estate Planning by and for the Really, Really, Rich (I don't they will like my
explaining this publically).**

So we have the poor with little to leave behind, and the middle class with something to
leave behind. All would like to leave their children something. How does the upper
class, especially the really, really rich, see it?

Let's suppose someone inherits $10,000,000 in stocks and bonds (after inheritance
taxes). Then there are the houses, the cars, and more, but let's just focus on the
$10,000,000. Depending on your perspective, that may be upper class or really, really,
rich (remembering that some estates are in the hundreds of millions or even billions of
dollars), but let's go with these nice round figures.

The $10,000,000 estate spins off 5% annual interest which is $500,000 to live on. That is tough, especially with taxes, but some people do seem to manage. If the individual inherits this at age 25 and reasonably expects to live to 75, perhaps 85, then it has to last a number of years. So we can expect 50-60 years of inflation during the individual's lifetime.

Do you know the Rule of 72? If you take 72 and divide any inflation rate into it, the result will be approximately how many years before inflation doubles.[39] An inflation rate of 2%-3% is generally average in a growing economy. Let's consider low inflation in a growing economy at 2%. Divide 72 by 2 and we get 36. So if our individual will need to live off this income for 50 years (without [horrors!] having to go to work himself), the individual will need $1,195,000 per year in the 50th year. Assuming dividend rates remain the same, the fortune will have to grow to $23,900,000 by the 50th year. (initial $10,000,000 plus $10,000,000 on the 36 multiple, and then $3,900,000 more for the remaining 14 years to total 50).

So as our individual doesn't have to work, and doesn't want to work, the challenge over 50 years is to grow the fortune by an additional 139% ($10,000,000 growing to $23,900,000). Let's assume our individual is very sharp on finances and doesn't need to pay for outside financial advisors. This is still a lot of increased wealth!

---

[39] Also this can be used to determine the number of years it would take to double your investment at any percentage of simple interest, and other uses.

And what about taxes? Our individual is struggling on $500,000 per year minus taxes. If this is all dividends, there can be some tax advantage on "qualified dividends," under the tax law but for the moment, let's say it's all taxable and our individual, with others likeminded, lobby Congress to reduce the tax on all dividends to zero (and state legislatures, too). So now there is $500,000 tax free. That should take a strain off the budget.

But how will these likeminded individuals successfully lobby for the tax cut? If they say, "those of who have to live on $500,000 per year without having to go to work are having a rough time" that won't sell with the public. So the argument would be, "this is to take the pressure of the senior citizens struggling to live on Social Security and some dividends on the little stock they own, and the pressure off the middle class trying to grow their retirement funds." But wait! Senior citizens who own investments generally do in IRAs and 401(k) or 401(b) plans. Likewise, the middle class doing the saving for retirement. Generally, this money is withdrawn as ordinary taxable income,[40] just as if it was earned on the job, and therefore is taxed, whether it came from dividends, interest, capital gains, or any other way. So reducing the tax on dividends to zero would have zero effect on most Americans' retirement savings, while they are accumulating or while they are withdrawing the money. But it would have a positive effect for multimillionaires who inherit most of their income **outside** of protected retirement funds. (Remember that no matter how much income anyone has, there are limits on how much can be put into those funds, but no limits on how much of one's income one can invest in ordinary

---

[40] The big exception is money in ROTH accounts, which are withdrawn tax free. These aren't for everyone, and like all retirement accounts, there are complexities, but I recommend that everyone should look into the possibility.

broker accounts. Also those contributions have to be from **earned** income (job) which many multimillionaires don't have in the first place. So there is generally very little of their fortune, if any, in protected retirement funds.)

I mentioned "capital gains" which are the profits on selling a security. You buy a share of stock worth $10 and sell it for $15. That is a capital gain.

Our individual will be trying to grow the fortune during his lifetime. Wouldn't it be nice it capital gains weren't taxed at all? The sales pitch on this would be the same as for dividends, but what is the reality?

Capital gains are generally taxed differently than ordinary income, but in a tax protected fund, they aren't taxed at all until withdrawal. Then they are taxed as ordinary income.[41] So tax cuts on capital gains don't affect capital gains for most Americans, but will be very advantageous for the upper class and especially the really, really, rich.

What about capital losses? That is when you buy the stock for $15 and sell it for $10, taking a $5 loss. You can take that $5 loss as a tax loss, **unless** it is in a retirement fund where that rule doesn't apply. There, you simply have $5 loss. But for our individual who has $10,000,000 (and growing!) in regular brokerage accounts, the $5 capital loss is a taxable deduction. But wait! If we have reduced dividends to zero and capital gains to zero, there is zero taxable income, so what good is the tax loss? Well, perhaps there is some other income that **is** taxable, such as interest on a bank account, or perhaps

---

[41] Although we still have the exception for ROTH funds.

income from a rental property. Anything to reduce taxes to zero, or as close to zero as possible.

What about the next generation? Let us say our individual has two children and they live in the mansion and wait many years until they inherit the estate. Neither they nor the parent know how long to plan for, but we do, so we will say the parent dies at 75, having lived on $1,195,000 of income in the final year, and leaving behind $23,900,000 in the estate. The children, by this time, are both 40 (we'll make them twins). But wait! $23,900,000 divided by two is $11,950,000 each, spinning off $597,500 each. We'll leave out the mansion and cars again, and focus on the money. Each of the children will have to live on half the income the parent did in the final year, or (in today's dollars) instead of living on $500,000 per year, they will have to get by on $250,000 per year. This means each one will have to reduce their lifestyle by 50% compared to the parent. How can we let this happen?

If each child, then, is to inherit a fortune that will enable each to live as well as the parent, then the estate has to double for each to receive half of that higher figure. This means that the parent has a mission throughout his lifetime to live only on the income from the estate, not sell a security (except to buy another one), and grow the fortune to $47,800,000 by age 75. This will enable each child to inherit $23,900,000, with $1,195,00 annual income each. Then they are just as well off as the parents and not have to cut corners. In the end, this is the equivalent in today's dollars of each one inheriting $10,000,000 and living off $500,000 per year. So the fortune hasn't grown enough that they can have a better lifestyle than the parent, but at least they are not moving backward. Many of the really, really, rich want to grow the fortune even more so that their children can have an even better life than they did (don't we all, though). So the cycle repeats.

We do want to emphasize that many of the upper class and really, really, rich give quite generously to charities as well as politicians and take up noble causes. But certainly (like the rest of us as individuals) they are trying to protect their self-interest as to taxes and otherwise (and have more leverage than the rest of us as individuals).

So if the obligation of the individual is not only make sure they live right off investment income and never pull living expenses out of the capital itself, but to make it grow to keep his income up with inflation, and provide for the next generation. In this instance our individual inherits $10,000,000 at age 25 and plans to make it grow so that over 50 years, should he die at 75, the fortune will have to grow to $47,800,000 just so the children don't have to cut back (and preferably more, so they can live even better!). But this is leaving out estate taxes.

Continuing to look only at the money, and leaving out the mansions, cars, etc.
The first $11,700,000 of the estate is nontaxable (remember, the poor and middle class can't use all of the exemption, but this estate can). So that means $36,100,000 of the estate is taxable. Since the estate is more than $1,000,000, there is that flat figure of

$345,800 to pay. So we need the estate to be at least $48,145,800 to be able to take the exemption ($11,700,000), and then pay the flat figure of $345,800 ($47,800,000 plus $345,800).

But wait! Over $1,000,000 there is an additional tax of 40% from there on up. So we have a tax to pay of $1,040,000 on the remaining $35,100,000 which means we need a total estate of $49,185,830[42] in order to take the exemption, pay the flat tax, pay the percentage tax and still be leaving enough behind for the next generation to do just as well (but no better!) than the previous. How unfair! That means the obligation of the parent is to multiply the fortune by almost 500%! Wouldn't it be great, wouldn't it be fantastic, if we eliminated the estate tax? That would save the estate $1.385,830 (not counting state taxes) and would be a little less pressure for the overstressed parent trying to make all this happen.

How can this argument be made? Because we already have the $11,700,000 exemption it is hard to say reducing all inheritance taxes to zero will help the poor and middle class. But then there is the argument that this will help create jobs…somehow (no Conservative Republican will tell how).

So the poor and middle class on the one hand, and the upper class and really, really, rich see wealth and estate planning totally differently, and for good reason.

---

[42] Mathematicians in the audience will see I am doing this arithmetically, not algebraically, so the figures are actually somewhat low, but that is for simplification. Mathematicians who are reading this chapter can run the figures algebraically in their spare time and enjoy reaching the exact figures.

Two Important Points to Note:

In 2001 the Republicans under George W. Bush passed legislation to phase out the estate tax, so that in calendar year 2010, there was none. That's right: zero. So if our individual's heirs were lucky enough for that person to die in 2010, there would be no taxes whatsoever on the multimillion dollar inheritance. Of course, the poor and middle class still paid full taxes on their earnings. The Republicans saw this as a wonderful, wonderful, thing. (Inheritance taxes then were restored in 2011.)

Also, if someone does not sell a stock by the time of death, there is no capital gains stock. So if someone buys $1,000,000 of stock and hangs on to it for 50 years to where it is worth $10,000,000 **but does not sell it in his lifetime**, capital gains tax is not applied. So it comes under estate tax only. If the lucky heirs inherit only the $10,000,000, then of course they pay no tax. The poor and middle class still pay full taxes on their earnings.

How far has this gotten? As far as: "we have to cut taxes on the top 1% because then they will be happy and create jobs. If the Democrats raise their taxes they will be mad and create jobs." But see "Jobs, Jobs, Jobs" for that discussion.

But what about cutting taxes on the middle class and poor? Those tax cuts have to be restricted because they have to be quite concerned about the mounting national debt. So the 2017 tax bill helped the rich, there were some tokens for the poor (some of which were indeed helpful, such as the increase in the standard deduction), and many middle class got tax increases (due in part to eliminating the personal exemption for those itemizing deductions). But in the first two Trump budgets (before COVID 19 hit), he and the Congressional Republicans[43] had still increased the deficit to approximately a trillion a year and made history!

"We need to cut taxes on business because then they will create jobs." Businesses largely used their tax cuts for stock buybacks rather than create jobs. Let's deal with the myth of the job creation first (Also see "Jobs, Jobs, Jobs.").

Suppose a Jason and I own a company that collects revenue of $10,000,000 this year for sales of goods or services and after paying our costs of rent or mortgage, utilities, inventory, supplies, and compensation to our employees (remembering that employees are a cost to a business), we have $1,000,000 worth of gross profit.[44]

Revenue minus sales equals gross profit. Gross profit minus taxes equals net profit.

At this time, the federal corporate tax is 21%[45] so let's go with that. Of our $1,000,000 gross profit, $210,000 goes for federal taxes. We'll leave out state income taxes, and say then that our net profit is $790,000. That leaves $395,000 for Jason and $395,000 for me.[46]

---

[43] Remember that in 2017 and 2018 the Republicans still controlled both houses of Congress as well as the Presidency. So they definitely cannot blame the Democrats for what they did.

[44] The accountants and financial analysts will refer to this as an Operating Ratio, or "OR" of 90, which is that 90% of our revenue constitutes expenses leaving 10% for gross profit.

[45] Remembering that corporate tax is different from individual income tax. Corporate tax is on gross profit. Individual tax is based on gross income minus deductions.

[46] If we are running our business well, and you are I are actively involved in its operations, we should also be collecting a salary but that is already accounted for within the employee compensation.

Now let's say the federal corporate tax drops to 0%. To create jobs, say the Conservative Republicans. Now the gross and net profit are the same $1,000,000, and that is $500,000 for you and $500,000 for me. (And we didn't have to do anything: we didn't have to increase sales, cut costs, and definitely not create jobs.) I vote we take the money. Jason says, "Oh, no. I am a Conservative Republican. The patriotic thing to do with a corporate tax cut is to create jobs. With that extra $210,000, we can create four jobs with total cost of $52,500 per year. Those will be nice jobs for someone who needs them."

I say, "but we don't have anything for them to do."

Jason says, "that matters not. When we get a tax cut, we use it to create jobs. That is Conservative Republican philosophy. The four new employees can stand around and watch the others work and collect their salary each week for doing so."

I say, "this is going to cause resentment among all the employees actually working."

But….what are the odds that Jason, even as a Conservative Republican, is going to oppose taking the extra money? I expect that no Conservative Republican will actually say that about his own corporate income tax cut.

How, then, are jobs created. In "Jobs, Jobs, Jobs" I point out that it is in response to demand or anticipated demand. Suppose we have an exciting new product idea and we anticipate much profit rolling in once we get it up and running. We need some development, proper packaging, and so on, so we hire four new employees to work on this. We have a motivation to hire. They each are a cost of $52,500 per year, which is $210,000. How does our accounting work now?

Revenue[47]	$10,000,000	Revenue	$10,000,000
Costs	- $ 9,210,000	Costs	- $ 9,210,000
Gross Profit	$ 790,000	Gross Profit	$ 790,000
Tax at 21%	- $ 165,900	Tax at 0%	- $ 0
Net Profit	$ 624,000	Net Profit	$ 790,000

So either way, the new employees cut into our profit, but we are willing to do this because we have high expectations for the profits that we will see once our exciting new product is fully ready and on the market. Either way, the tax cut flows into our pocket. The difference between the 21% and 0% columns is no longer $210,000 because the tax at 21% is now $165,900. The reason for that is that the employee costs are a new expense, affecting our gross profit. Note, however, we have managed to cut our own taxes by $44,100 ($210,000-$165,900) at the 21% tax rate as a result.

"Death Tax"

---

[47] Remembering that for this example, we do not yet have the new product and therefore have no sales of it. So revenue is unaffected at this point.

Somewhere along the line, Conservative Republicans decided to try renaming the estate tax altogether. How far did this go? It got to where I told a one, "if there is a tax on dying, then I refuse to pay it and therefore will not be allowed to die and will be eternal." The reply I got was, "the death tax is a secret tax implemented by Bill Clinton[48] that the public doesn't know about. The funeral director has to add it into the bill or you can't have a funeral and be buried. It is hidden in with the other costs on the invoice because the funeral director can't let you know about it."

Dividends and Buybacks

So corporations can distribute the money saved from tax cuts to stockholders as dividends. The Conservative Republicans will say this is to help the middle class struggling to accumulate more financial resources to serve them in their retirement years, and for those already retired who are struggling. But wait. Are these the people the Conservative Republicans are really trying to help? No, they are trying to help the top 1%.

Most retirement savings are in 401(k), 403(b), or IRA accounts which are tax deferred. This means that the money is put into the account and income taxes only apply when the money is withdrawn. So someone has significant retirement savings, having put money away regularly, and let the capital gains and dividends accumulate. So they have retired with $1,000,000 and want to withdraw out $50,000 this year. Or $10,000, or $100,000. How is the income tax applied? The money (only as it is withdrawn) is taxed

---

[48] Of course, no President "implements" a tax. This has to be an Act of Congress which the President can sign, or can veto, subject to Congress passing it over his veto.

the same as "regular income" which is the percentage applied to wages. So cutting

taxes on dividends or capital gains, even to zero, doesn't have any effect. If the

retirement savings are in a ROTH account, then the money being withdrawn isn't taxed

anyway, so the tax cuts on dividends and capital gains still don't apply.

Where, then, do the tax cuts, even to zero, ever apply? They apply to dividends and

capital gains held outside a protected account. That is, you can walk into any

stockbroker in the United States, and simply open a stock account. Put in an opening

deposit and you can buy and sell stocks on the open market. You can have capital

gains, capital losses, and dividends, and each one is what accountants (and the IRS)

call a "taxable event." An event has occurred that affects your taxes. (In the particular

retirement accounts mentioned above, there are zero taxable events until the money is

withdrawn, and here again the ROTH is an exception.)

Well, do middle class Americans and retired Americans have taxable brokerage

accounts. Sure, many do. But is this about them? Consider the poorest person in the

country, perhaps, unfortunately, homeless and truly destitute. Then consider the

wealthiest person in the country? These are the two extremes. Who do you believe

owns the most stock in a taxable brokerage account? Draw a line and put the poorest

person on one end and the wealthiest person on the other. Where would you place

yourself on the line? Where would you place most Americans? So these tax cuts **can**

benefit some people who are not wealthy, but not all, as many people do not have

taxable stock brokerage accounts to begin with. Many have difficulty funding their established retirement accounts mentioned above. Suppose someone in the middle class has managed to put money away in a taxable brokerage account for many years, and now has $100,000 in stock. Some of his investments pay dividends, some not.[49] Let us say $50,000 worth of her stock is paying a 3% dividend. That is $1,500 per year. Tax the dividends or don't tax the dividends, we still aren't talking about a lot of money.

But consider the person who has $10,000,000 in stock, perhaps even inherited, and half of the stock pays the same dividend. That is $150,000 per year. If that is tax free, that can make a difference.

Buybacks

What else can a company do with tax cuts? We see that the first choice will not be to create jobs. With a public company (traded on the stock market, versus privately held, where a family or a small group of investors own all the stock), they can buy back stock that has already been issued.

So we have a company that over time has issued 1,000,000 shares of stock and today, as the company has grown, and become more profitable, the stock is worth $100 per share. This means the "market capitalization" is $100,000,000.[50]

---

[49] Many companies in rapid growth do not pay dividends, but reinvest the money in the growth of the company. In the end, they do not show a profit because after reinvesting in buildings, machines, and, yes, people, there is little or nothing left to show as profit, therefore there is nothing to pay out as a dividend and there are little if any income taxes (because income taxes are on gross profit). Amazon, for example, has never paid a dividend as of this writing, but the company, and the value of the stock, have grown nicely.

[50] The accountants explain that this is the total value of the company in the opinion of the stock market—right now. Today. And this can fluctuate by the minute if the market is open, as stocks go up and come down by the minute. The concept that is if you were to step forward and offer to buy every share of stock in the company—this minute—you would need $100,000,000 to buy it all, because that's what the market

What if the company wanted to expand, and instead of borrowing the money to do so, the board of directors decided to issue more stock. Tomorrow they issue an additional 1,000,000 shares, so the value of each share of stock is now diluted. There are now 2,000,000 shares in existence, and the company is the same company, so the share of each stock should now drop to a value of $50.00, to the distaste of many stockholders. Some bought the stock at $100 hoping it would go up, and now it has gone down to $50.00 per share. [51] If the company's expansion is successful, it might be a $400,000,000 company somewhere down the road, but first it has to double to bring those stockholders back to where they were, and this could take many years before the company advances further. Still, the company has no loan to pay back, and no interest, so this might be the best decision by the board of directors. Some might decide to do half and half ("equity financing" and "debt financing").

What if there were only 500,000 shares? The company is still the same company, so the stock should now be worth twice the $100 price, so, $200 per share. What if there were only 950,000 shares instead of 1,000,000? Then the value of each share should increase 1.0526%[52] So the board of directors could decide to take $5,000,000 of tax cut

(sellers and buyers, supply and demand), have established as the value of the company—this minute—and therefore the appropriate price for the entire company (all of the stock).

[51] Wouldn't it be great if you knew the day before what was going to happen tomorrow? You might have some inside information, sell the stock at $100, and buy it back tomorrow at $50. However, this is what is called insider trading, and you can end up in federal prison for years. This is where ambition is replaced by greed, and some people with millions already in their pockets do this sort of thing because "this much isn't enough). (Note also the goal of taking care of the next generation, as discussed above.) Some sharp people, however, do examine corporate reports, *The Wall Street Journal*, and other resources available to the general public and make some very good guesses. Some very highly paid people at some of the Wall Street firms do very well by focusing on one company or industry and can put the available pieces of the jigsaw puzzle together, and conclude "what the whole picture must look like." The successful result can raise suspicions at the Securities and Exchange Commission but still, being very smart and doing meticulous research isn't against the law.

money and "buyback" 50,000 of the 1,000,000 shares outstanding, at $100 per share.

(50,000 times $100 = $5,000,000). The stock remaining should now immediately jump

by 1.0526% to $105.26 per share.

Why would the board of directors do this? It makes the stockholders already in the

game very happy. They have a 5.26% immediate profit and they didn't have to do

anything. Nor did the company. The company did not have to introduce a new product,

buy new building or machines, or have to create new jobs and bring in any new

employees (remember the demand for the product hasn't changed, so production

doesn't have to change).

Who holds most of the stock in the company? Some middle class investors may own

the stock, in or out of retirement accounts. Some employees may own some.[53]

But do you think large chunks of the stock may be owned by members of the board of

directors and members of the top 1% personally. Examine the publically available

reports filed with the Securities and Exchange Commission

(https://www.sec.gov/edgar/searchedgar/companysearch.html) which will show the

holdings of board members, and anyone else who owns 5% or more of the stock. These

are the people who will most benefit. This doesn't mean this in itself is wrong, but let's

---

[52] 950,000 divided by 1,000,000 = 1.0526%. **Not** 1,000,000 divided by 950,000 which gives us 95% but is computing in the other direction.

[53] Many large companies have ESOP (Employee Stock Ownership Programs). Employees can buy stock in the company, often by regular payroll deduction, and sometimes at a discount from the market price. It is often a very good financial decision for employees to participate and, from the company's point of view, it gives the employee a vested interest in making the company more successful, above and beyond their own salary, wages, and any other direct composition. The employee **wants** the stock to go up.

see things as they are and not the way the Conservative Republicans want us to think they are.

Yet it is worth mentioning that this was a criticism of some companies. These are companies who benefited from the 2008 bailout funds; made large profits during the Obama years when business was good, and were asking for more federal government aid in 2020. What happened to all the profits? In some cases, they went for stock buybacks. Many people made a lot of money as their stock suddenly increased. But prudent management would dictate that some profits should beheld (as "retained earnings") to help the company through rougher times when they come along.

China and Tariffs, and Mexico, Too!

Myths:

"China has stolen jobs from the United States."

"China has stolen our technology."

"Raising tariffs are the answer. That brings money from China into the U.S. Treasury."

"We can force China to stop manipulating its currency."

"China has stolen jobs from the United States."

This is hard to believe. If I give you a dollar, did you steal it from me? No? Let's start with that.

Does a U.S. company send a job to China? Not as much as a job is eliminated here and brought into existence over there to fill the same demand.[54] So we'll say production is moved over.

We have a U.S. company that has 100 employees turning out a product in the U.S. But it would be cheaper to have the work done in China. Senior management calculates that with the lower cost, the long cargo transportation route to the U.S. plus any customs duties and other expenses will still be cheaper than a U.S. manufacture.[55]

Does the company actually ship a job over? No, a job is eliminated here and a new one comes into existence there, whether it is China, or someplace else.[56]

---

[54] See "Socialism and Capitalism."

[55] Historically, and similarly, we had a movement of production from the northeastern U.S. states to the southern U.S. states beginning shortly after midcentury, because labor costs were lower in the South. This is capitalism.

[56] The other side of the coin is where some manufacturers decide it is cheaper (more profitable) to move production **into** the United States. Daimler (Mercedes) moved some into Tuscaloosa, Alabama, and BMW moved some into Spartanburg, South Carolina. So these are jobs eliminated in Germany and brought into existence in the United States because the production has been moved. The reason remains cutting costs and the motivation remains the profit motive. Part of the concept was that this way, the completed car is closer to the buyer (lower transportation costs for the finished product).

Is there a theft by China involved here? No, it is a voluntary movement of production by a capitalist enterprise pursuing the profit motive. I am not critical. That's capitalism. I like to see companies make a profit rather than a loss. I like to see Americans have jobs, too. How to reconcile? Read on.

Narrative #1:

An interesting narrative is that of Carrier in Indianapolis, Indiana. In 2016, before taking office, President-Elect Trump and Vice President-Elect Pence went to the Carrier factory which had been talking about relocating some production to Mexico. There was a major press conference where Trump announced that he had convinced Carrier to keep the jobs right there. He made believe he was quite a salesman! I say "made believe" because what didn't get maximum publicity was that it was –ahem—arranged that they would receive $7,000,000 in economic incentives, such as state tax breaks, for staying. Mike Pence was still Governor of Indiana at the time.[57]

The Conservative Republicans went on and on about how hundreds of jobs had been saved by Donald Trump, and he wasn't even in office yet! How wonderful! Imagine how great he will be once he is President! But the end of the story is that the jobs left anyway, by 2018.[58] No press conference. And, no, they didn't give the money back, either.

---

[57] https://time.com/4588349/donald-trump-carrier-jobs-speech/
[58] https://www.popularmechanics.com/technology/infrastructure/a20066498/carrier-factory-donald-trump-jobs/

So this was quite a publicity stunt, but that seems to be all it was ever designed to be.[59]

<sigh>

Narrative #2:

Donald Trump said in 2016 that he would create millions of new coal-mining jobs.[60] But

really, how many new jobs are there as of 2020? Jobs in the coal mines have continued

to diminish all along.[61] He said, as about many other things, "I know how to get it done."

But he would not tell how. He still will not tell. He didn't get it done. A promise made, a

promise broken.

What are the fundamentals here? Let's go back to 1941. My grandfather bought the

house I grew up in, and immediately changed the furnace from coal to oil. Each method

boiled water to steam, which went through the pipes to the radiators. Years later, when I

came along, he explained that with a coal furnace, you have to add coal periodically.

This met setting the alarm to get up in the middle of the night to add coal. Coal was dirty

to handle and would raise a cloud of black dust when it was delivered to the house. Oil,

on the other hand, had this amazing device called a thermostat that would start the

furnace when the temperature went below the setting. Oil, stored in a tank, would begin

---

[59] Trump had made a threat that there would be a new 35% tax on imports from Mexico for U.S. companies that moved their production to Mexico. So the message was that this would apply to Carrier. https://money.cnn.com/2016/12/04/investing/donald-trump-tax-jobs/index.html But it would not apply to products of companies such as Rheem which were already producing in Mexico. But in the end it didn't matter because the tax never became law. President Donald J. Trump talked it up in the 2016 campaign but never sent the bill to Congress. I can find no record that the bill he emphasized as a top priority was ever written. Many Conservative Republicans were enthusiastic about it in 2016 but seemed to have forgotten about it by 2017.
[60] https://www.cnbc.com/2016/11/22/cramer-on-trumps-energy-pledge-there-are-no-millions-of-jobs-that-can-be-created.html
[61] https://www.forbes.com/sites/chuckjones/2020/08/26/trumps-coal-resurgence-promise-has-gone-underground/?sh=29019ced56d8

to flow to the furnace via a pump, be turned into a spray, a fire would ignite, and direct flame would heat the water. Also it was cheaper. So, more efficient, cleaner, and cheaper—how hard is to choose? (Some large commercial operations use conveyor belts and are staffed 24/7.)

Coal is being used less and less. In fact oil is sometimes being replaced by natural gas for the same reasons oil replaced coal in so many uses. So if we need less and less coal, how can an argument be made that someone knows how (but will not tell) to create millions of new coal mining jobs?

Then we have technology which is getting more efficient all the time. I don't know much about mining, but the trade journal, *Mining Technology* does, and they say technology in mining is advancing rapidly.[62] This means fewer miners needed to produce the same amount of coal.

So here is a combination: we need fewer miners to produce the same amount of coal and less coal is needed. Demand drives supply which creates a need for someone to fill a job **but** technology is a consideration also.

How did Trump plan to create millions of new coal mining jobs given the above? The only way would be to increase demand faster than technology eliminated jobs. Perhaps

---

[62] https://www.mining-technology.com/features/featureten-technologies-with-the-power-to-transform-mining-4211240/

coal-fired jet airplanes? Coal-fired air conditioners? He would not tell. He still will not tell. He didn't get it done. A promise made, a promise broken.

Technology

Before returning to China and Tariffs, which is where we started, let's revisit technology for a moment. I said above I like businesses to make a profit, and I like people to have jobs. But regardless of demand, technology gets in the way. True, someone has a job designing and producing the technology, whether hardware or software, but the technology only replaces a person if it will be a cost savings (increase profit).

Example A: Technology costs $1,000,000 and has an expected useful life of ten years. It will replace one employee who costs $50,000 per year. If we replace the employee, we will lose $500,000 over ten years. If we keep the employee, we save $500,000 over ten years. We aren't counting the $500,000 twice, but looking at it from two different points of view, but the result is the same: the technology is a bad investment. You wouldn't buy it.

Example B: Technology costs $100,000 and has an expected useful life of ten years. It will replace one employee who costs $50,000 per year. If we replace the employee, we will save $400,000 over ten years. If we keep the employee, we lose $400,000 over ten years. You would buy the technology (or answer to the stockholders about why you are wasting the company's money that they could be getting in dividends).

The business should also consider how long before the technology becomes obsolete. Technology is moving so fast that while this has a useful life of ten years, it may be superseded by new technology in five. Then we'll have to buy the new version anyway, to keep up with the competition that is bringing the new technology online. But we may be able to see the first technology to someone else, perhaps in a less developed country (LDC) where a business cannot afford the very latest thing. All this is a matter of estimating, trying to predict the future, but for our discussion to be complete, I've introduced it here.

On a larger level, considering the national economy, we may want to consider how it affects the big picture. Let's call this a self-checkout technology that has appeared in grocery stores, hardware stores, and other retail businesses. If we are looking at the national economy, we would have a question about where the technology is developed and produced (in the U.S.? China?). The retailer could be eliminating a job (cost) in the United States, but not bringing an equivalent job into China. The jobs eliminated here would be a relatively low wage retail cashier's job, and the jobs in China would be higher paid high-tech jobs (relatively speaking, as China's wages are lower than in the U.S., which we'll address further).

But a wage earner at a low income level usually has difficulty finding a new job. A retail sales clerk may only know how to be a retail sales clerk. Apply for another job as a retail sales clerk? But as self-checkout technology has become more and more prevalent, fewer and fewer retail sales clerk jobs are available. This can mean a welfare application from someone who is willing to work, and work hard, but lived paycheck to paycheck even while working fulltime. We can also consider online shopping on the one hand (eliminating) and population growth on the other hand (demand for more retail sales) but we'll leave that to the professional economists to try to measure and to argue over. The principle is clear.

Also it is clear that if this technology is being designed and produced outside the United States, then it is the high-tech job growth that is helping the foreign economy. This helps spur more growth in the foreign economy. But if the technology is designed and produced inside the United States, then the high-tech job growth happened here, but we have the social problem of eliminating jobs for people who are prone to facing very hard times, and for long periods, while bringing into existence jobs for the more highly educated. We need both.

A Digression Into Republican Solutions

The Republican solution for the people towards the bottom of the economy is to decrease help. A clear example was Reagan's push, during the First Reagan Recession, to cut food stamps while unemployment increased.[63]

This was around the time the Conservative Republicans started setting thresholds for taxing Social Security benefits which previously had been exempt from federal income

---

[63] https://www.nytimes.com/1982/08/25/us/reagan-s-social-impact-news-analysis.html

taxes.[64] Prior to Ronald Reagan, no one ever paid federal income taxes on their Social Security payment. Today, many senior citizens people do, and the average Social Security payment for retirees as of November, 2020 was $1,449.78 total.[65] Yes, there are those who receive more, but this is an average, so there are those who receive less. This wasn't addressed in the "Tax Cuts and Jobs Act of 2017" and presumably the Conservative Republicans still to this day see the tax on Social Security benefits to be a wonderful, wonderful thing.[66]

Production, Capitalism, Trade Secrets, and Patents

So production moves to where the costs will be lower. This takes into consideration all compensation (wages, medical insurance,[67] paid holidays and vacations, tuition reimbursement, retirement funds and whatever else). Some countries will have some costs that other countries do not and a cost can be higher in one country than another. Overall, much more complicated than many conservatives realize. Good business planners take all these factors in consideration.

I mentioned above about some production moving from north to south within the United States, and some foreign production moving into the United States. But what about

---

[64] https://www.ssa.gov/history/taxationofbenefits.html

[65] https://www.ssa.gov/policy/docs/quickfacts/stat_snapshot/

[66] I have another chapter, "Social Security and Medicare," but this seemed like a good place to briefly discuss these particular Conservative Republican policies.

[67] Note that while group medical insurance is a factor in many [not all] companies, in many countries there is a government-based medical insurance [coverage] or medicine [care} in part or whole. Here it isn't a direct company or employee expense, but is taxpayer-funded. Still, higher taxes on the companies and individuals are needed to cover the cost. Hence, the foreign producer may have to cover lower wages but higher taxes.

China (and perhaps other countries) being accused of "stealing" patents and trade secrets.

Let's define our term. If someone forces you to turn over your watch, that is stealing. If you give me your watch voluntarily, that is not stealing. So let's proceed with that. Is China forcing U.S. companies to turn over patents and trade secrets? Or are the U.S. companies **voluntarily** turning them over when they move production?

Let's note also that patents are public information.[68] So if someone wants to copy someone else's product that is patented, the patent is public information. But is it possible to copy a product from looking at the patent? Sometimes. Sometimes it is possible to take a product, say an amazing new computer mouse, disassemble it, determine how it is made and copy it. We don't need to look at the patent. To avoid a patent infringement case, we may make some adjustments in our amazing new computer mouse, so cannot to be said to be the same thing (patent infringement).

Perhaps the amazing new computer mouse isn't patented or patentable in the first place. We need to have a new and different article to be considered for patenting. Generally, it should be new, unique, useful, and not previously obvious. It may be a new twist on the existing idea which, if it can't be patented, will thus have no patent protection. So anyone could copy it.

---

[68] They have to be, because if we want to patent something, first we do a patent search to see if there already may be a patent on what we came up with on our own. If patents weren't public, how could anyone be forewarned that there are infringing on a protected idea?

When can the patent, then, fully protected? We have a new pharmaceutical. We display the chemical structure in our patent application which will become public information. What we don't include is the process: how much a particular component has to be heated and for how long before being combined with another one, for example. That is our trade secret. Someone can examine the patent at great length and still be making guesses as to exactly how our pharmaceutical is produced.

Some articles are never patented because the patent would be public information and someday the patent protection would expire. So they are kept trade secrets. Coca-Cola is an example: the syrup formula and process have been kept a trade secret and never has been patented. In this case, there is no legal protection, and while there are other cola drinks, it seems to have not been possible for anyone to break down the syrup to determine the exact components, quantities, and process, and duplicate the exact product.

Where does this bring us? China has very weak patent protection laws to begin with. They base this on Karl Marx's idea that knowledge should be freely available to everyone.[69] (China is very good at being capitalistic when that is convenient and communistic when that is convenient.)

So to sum it up: if a U.S. company takes a patented idea, a process, a trade secret, and teaches a foreign company how to make the product, then they know how to make the

---

[69] The U.S. concept, from originally providing for patents in the Constitution, to the present day, is that some protection is necessary, granting exclusive rights to an inventor, in order to encourage people to invent things. This gives them a temporary monopoly to recoup their costs and make a profit.

product. You can't take that back if you move your production back home. If, then, that company is located in a country with weak patent protection, you may be completely out of luck.

Remember what I said above about "good business planners?" Ahem. Any good business planner will understand that above paragraph and understand the risks of moving the production to China. A lousy business planner will not understand that above paragraph and take the risks without understanding that they are there. An unethical business planner will understand the risks, be happy to take the bonus for the extra profits gained, and be delighted to blame someone else when product and process are copied.

How to encourage U.S. companies to keep production in the U.S.? It is by discouraging companies from moving production outside the U.S. We could have legislation or regulation stating that X, Y, and Z pharmaceuticals must be available for inspection by the U.S. Food and Drug Administration at a facility **within** the United States at every stage of production. Therefore, the production would have to stay here. We can expect that other countries will retaliate with some restriction on something on their side, but this is the back-and-forth that is expected among countries and governments in a globalized society.[70]

---

[70] Some conservatives say, "The problem is globalization. I am against globalization." Rarely can they define it, but more importantly, when I ask "how will you convince every country in the world to move backwards?" they cannot answer that. So we will deal with globalization as something that is, and what we can do to minimize our losses and maximize our gains (as is every other country trying to do) rather than talk about eliminating something and taking no action at all in our favor (which seems to be conservative agenda).

But important to note: the Conservative Republicans say we are better off with fewer regulations on business so that businesses can do what they want.[71]

We saw during the early stages of the Coronavirus Pandemic that some needed medical articles were being exported from the United States and hence not available here in sufficient quantities.[72] Note that above paragraph about keeping production here. But even with production here, the United States is a huge exporter. What to do?

The President, as head of the Executive Branch, has substantial authority to restrict exports. Generally:

Step A: declare something a controlled article.

Step B: instruct the enforcement agencies to deny all licenses for this controlled article for the time being.[73]

There! This isn't oversimplified. This is the answer. President Trump decided not to do this.

The Republicans have not taken productive action to bringing production and jobs back to the United States, or protecting the public health. To do so would involve regulating businesses. It is a conservative principle that the fewer regulations on business, the

---

[71] See "Cut Regulations to Help Business and Help America."

[72] https://www.usatoday.com/story/news/investigations/2020/04/02/us-exports-masks-ppe-china-surged-early-phase-coronavirus/5109747002/ An interesting Congressional Research Service report is at https://crsreports.congress.gov/product/pdf/IF/IF11551

[73] As per authority in 50 United States Code 4812 at: https://www.law.cornell.edu/uscode/text/50/4812

better. "Business runs best when it makes its own decisions without the government being involved." But that leaves it purely to the profit motive, not always in the public interest.[74] This does not prevent the Republicans from making promises that they will bring production and jobs back, or protect the public health. They just don't like to keep those promises as it goes against their conservative philosophy.

But if we change a law or regulation to prevent a company from moving production elsewhere, or exporting, can this interfere with a contract? Yes. Can it interfere with contract law? No.

For there to be a contract it has to be a legal bargain.[75] If, then, carrying out the contract will be illegal, then the contract can be considered null and void, and no longer a contract. Of course, if an export license is now required and cannot be obtained, the U.S. company would return any money already collected, but would not be able to ship the now-controlled medical articles. The good business planner, referred to above, would not agree to an export contract unless there was a provision like: "this contract is subject to compliance with U.S. export laws and regulations in effect at the time and will be null and void if we cannot fulfill the contract in such compliance."

---

[74] See "Regulations."
[75] This is common law in the United States and most developed countries. We can have agreements to do lots of things, but that doesn't necessarily mean they are contracts. Contracts are enforceable at law. There is no such thing as an "invalid contract" in practice. If it is a contract, it is a contract that is enforceable at law. If it some other type of agreement, it is not a contract at all.

While this book isn't about solutions, the direction to take is government regulation. See the chapter "Cut Regulations to Help Business and Help America" for a discussion of government regulation.

Jobs, Jobs, Jobs

Myths:

"The role of business is to create jobs."

"Supply creates its own demand" (Say's Law).

Business and Jobs

What is the real purpose of a business? In grade school social studies, we learned that it was to try to make a profit (no guarantees, some business ventures look good but lose money). In the business schools of our universities, they teach that the purpose of a business is to maximize the owners' wealth (stockholders, partners in a partnership, or, often in small businesses, one owner—a sole proprietor).

It is true that as a national goal, we want to see jobs created, preferably good jobs with chances for advancement, and see them created here (having nothing against people in another country having jobs as well). But that is not the goal of a business. Business tries to avoid creating jobs in order to work towards the real goal, of **maximizing** the owners' wealth.

Example: in Phoenix, we have the Arizona Cardinals football team which used to be the St. Louis Cardinals. Many people say, "the football team creates jobs. There is the stadium and surrounding it are many chain and local restaurants that weren't there before. They are there because the stadium brings in thousands of people, many of whom want to have dinner before the game. There you are."

But where are we? Let's go to the football game today. I just got a bonus, so I'll take all of us and we'll have a nice dinner together, I'll pay for parking and admission, and we'll have our hot dogs and beer. We provide the demand (the desire + the ability to pay) and capitalism provides the services in response.

But wait! What if the socialist[76] football stadium was never built? Then we don't have the restaurants, parking attendants, food vendors inside the stadium, and no professional

---

[76] More about this in "Socialism and Capitalism."

football players drawing their salaries. How sad! Should I take my bonus and tear it up and flush it down into the sewer?

If desire + ability to pay is there, then we are going to take our demand and search for a supply. Possibly we will go downtown to dinner and a play. Or, to dinner and a concert. One way or another, if the funds are there and there is a desire to spend them on entertainment, we will find something to do.

"But wait!" say the conservatives. "Those restaurants were already there." That's true. But taking just the restaurants as our model, if we went to the restaurants near a football stadium, then we don't also go to the restaurant downtown. If there are 20 of us, then we will have dinner in 20 places, but not both. The demand has simply shifted from the restaurants near the stadium (which in our model now don't exist), to downtown. They will be busier than if demand was diverted elsewhere, and need lots of employees. Bring back the football stadium and the surrounding restaurants, and the restaurants downtown will be less busy and possibly plan some layoffs.

In this model, demand stays the same because the ability to pay (buying power) remains the same. The desire can be to go to a dinner and a football game one night, dinner and a play the next night, dinner and a concert the next night, and so on every night of the year. Alas! I don't have the ability to pay for all of that.

The conservatives count on the stadium and new restaurants being very visible to the public, and yes, new jobs being created, and on the lesser business elsewhere being so spread out around the community, with this and that restaurant laying off one or two people, not being so visible. They focus on the very visible jobs being created when that fits their agenda, but not on the corresponding layoffs.

So what creates jobs? Demand, not investment. It is true we need the investment to build the stadium and the new restaurants, but that is based on demand, or anticipated demand. That is, an investor may back a new restaurant near the football stadium because so many restaurants are full before the games that people are being turned away (supply can't accommodate demand), or if a new venue is being planned, expect that a new restaurant in the neighborhood could be profitable (anticipating future demand).

A specific retail example: here we have Jason who is an active tennis player and bought tennis balls at the Sports Authority for years. Sports Authority went bankrupt in 2016. Alas! has Jason not been able to buy tennis balls all this time because his supplier is not there anymore. Is this true? Does Jason have an alternative, such as Dick's Sporting Goods,[77] or the sporting goods departments at Target or Walmart? Of course; the demand is there so the supply will be there. These remaining retailers, and more, will each be able to sell somewhat more tennis balls over time.

---

[77] It is interesting to note that Dick's Sporting Goods bought the rights to the Sport Authority brand name, and other rights, at the Sports Authority bankruptcy auction (https://www.wsj.com/articles/dicks-sporting-goods-wins-sports-authority-brand-name-in-bankruptcy-auction-1467299379). At this time, the http://sportsauthority.com site redirects to Dick's Sporting Goods. It will be interesting to see what else they may decide to do with those rights.

But the closing of the Sports Authority and the elimination of jobs in that retail chain are much more visible to the public than jobs that were brought into existence in the other retailers, to handle their increased sales due to the increased demand they are seeing: one full timer here, one part-timer there, and so on. These other retailers will invest in more employees but only as the demand requires it.

Investment, then, responds to demand, or anticipated demand. [78]

Businesses Don't Want to Create Jobs.

Well, let's look at this in reverse. Why would a business want to create a job? Jobs are a cost. Business wants to bring in as much money as possible (revenue) and cut costs as much as possible (expense) in order to maximize profit, and, hence, the owners' wealth. There is a balancing act about not raising prices to where consumers run to a competitor and revenue ends up going down, and keeping staffing high enough so customers receive the quality and service they expect. Although, then, too, we have differences in expectations by consumers from Trader Joe's versus Costco; some consumers go to both.

I have a friend who sells on Amazon and eBay. He buys some novelty products by the carton and sells them one at a time. He is retired, and this is a nice little part time business he runs by himself. He has no employees because he has nothing for an employee to do, and he does not want to expand the business.

---

[78] See "Cut Taxes on the Top 10%"

But wait! According to Conservative Republican ideology, he should want to hire two, three, four people, because according to them, the role of his business is to create jobs. But that means his role is fundamentally not to make a profit, but to create jobs instead. He makes a profit rather than spend the money on employees he doesn't need.

Here we have a convenience store with two employees on duty at all times, 24 hours a day. Why don't they have 40 or 50 employees running around? Because two is all they need. One is the cashier while the other one tends to inventory and other duties. The second takes over as cashier when the regular cashier goes on break. That's all they need. To hire more people they don't need would interfere with profit. Demand drives supply of employees.

Suppose we have a warehouse operation that has been running smoothly with 100 employees. Inventory is in order, and customer shipments are made on time. The warehouse manager retires and a new warehouse manager is hired. He keeps everything running smoothly, and management is satisfied as that is what the manager is supposed to do.

Now that manager leaves and a new manager comes in. This manager gradually streamlines the operation until there are only 90 employees, and everything is still running smoothly. She goes to senior management to say, "those employees were averaging a cost to the company of $50,000 per year and I am therefore saving the company $500,000 per year with everything still getting done right and on time. How much bonus do I get?" This may well be a $250,000 bonus (50% of the first year's extra profit).

This manager stays a year, takes the bonus, and then quits for another job. Someone else is hired. He reports to senior management: "I don't know she did this all with only 90 employees, or how her predecessor did it with only 100. I have had to hire 10 more people to get it all done." That is a loss of $500,000 savings that was going right to profit, and an additional cost of $500,000 that is coming out of profit. This manager is costing the company $1,000,000 extra per year. He is quickly discharged and senior management searches for someone who can get it all done with 90 people, because they now that this is now possible.

So business wants to eliminate jobs as much as possible, and create them as little as possible.

But What About Say's Law?

This is often summarized as "supply creates its own demand" which is oversimplification. This is the foundation of conservative economics but is overapplied.

Consider the paper clip. We use fewer paper clips all the time because we are using less paper. We go into Staples and OfficeMax and generally can buy all the paper clips we need. Perhaps sometimes someone will go in and need a large supply and buy out the shelf. Perhaps another time paper clips will sit on the shelf for a week with no buyers. But overall, there is no paper clip shortage and no huge surplus of unsold paper clips produced and left unsold piling up in the warehouses somewhere (if that was so, the paper clip manufacturers would correct operations and make fewer paper clips until they unloaded the surplus).

So with ebbs and flows, we can consider that supply and demand of paper clips tend to be in balance.

According to supply-side economics, misapplying Say's Law, all we have to do is produce more paper clips (supply increases) and people will buy more (demand increase to match supply). But note above about the concept of huge supplies of unsold product in warehouses.

Do you have some money to invest? Let's invest it. Let's build ten factories to make paper clips. We'll buy the machinery and hire the people (anticipated demand), and off we go. We create a million paper clips for the market each day in each factory. Now the marketplace, which is stabilized, will become unstable because of excess supply. In order to move product, our competitors may reduce prices, and we will reduce prices as well, causing a price war. But have we done anything to create additional demand for paper clips?

No, the same people need the same number today that they would if our factories existed or not. (We will allow that some people will buy extra paper clips at a lower price not because they need more, but because they see the opportunity to stock up while the price is low.)

What do we do with the oversupply? Now we can pay to build the storage warehouses to hold millions and millions of unsold paper clips piling up each day until the day we give up on the whole idea.

Then is Say's Law wrong? No, but it has to be properly applied. Above is a misapplication. Here is a proper application:

Someone in Los Angeles would like to visit relatives in New York City but doesn't have enough vacation time to drive there and back and spend any realistic time at the destination. Rail, too. So air transportation is considered, but is ruled out as too expensive. So that rules out the trip.

But suppose an airline has unfilled seats on the Los Angeles→New York City flights (excess supply for the existing demand) and decides to cut prices. Or suppose several airlines do the same and cause a price war. As prices go down, our would-be traveler decides that the trip is now affordable a buys a round trip ticket to enjoy a nice visit with the relatives.

The supply has created demand but in the process of an **oversupply** causing a **price reduction** in a situation where there is a **flexible demand**. The flexible demand exists for airline tickets (and also considering rail and driving options), but only minutely for paper clips (stocking up).

So Say's Law can apply, but must be properly applied, not misapplied. The way the Conservative Republicans misapply it, is they come to a conclusion first and then try to determine a reason why their conclusion is correct, which is working backwards.

See also "China and Tariffs and Mexico, too!" for discussion as to U.S. production moving offshore, and some information regarding export controls.

Donald Trump Was a Business Success

Myths:

"Donald Trump was a great business success."

 "Therefore he will be a great president."

"He was a great builder."

Two at Once

Well, first, let's combine and address the first two as one, greater myth. Because someone is good at one thing doesn't mean he is good at something else. An already good tennis player can be a good badminton player from day one, yes, because the games, the eye-hand coordination, and so on are not completely different. This doesn't mean an already good tennis player can be a good football player from day one.

Business and Government

Are the skills of business and government more similar or more different? Well, in business we seek to make a profit[79] by charging those who receive the goods or services we have for sale[80] but in government we seek to provide a needed service whether it is profitable or not. There is a hurricane and FEMA[81] comes in to help with the recovery. The victims are not charged directly for FEMA's services; the taxpayers as a whole pay for the services. The services will be available for us, too, and we hope, like with the local fire department, we will not need them. But we are providing them for the public good, when local resources are overwhelmed. And we have a peace of mind that something is there to backup local resources in case our area is hit with a disaster. So there is a benefit for some, a potential benefit for others, and the government is seeking to cover its costs, not make a profit. (Business has an agenda of making a profit, but government's agenda is to break even.) [82]

In the corporate world, the stockholders elect the board of directors which then appoints the corporate officers (president, vice-president, etc.). In a closely held business like

---

[79] See "Jobs, Jobs, Jobs," and "Cut Regulations to Help Business and America"
[80] Although, in some situations, such as health coverage, the person receiving the services is not always the person paying the bill. If we have insurance through a third party (other than ourselves and the provider), we may have a deductible or a copay, but the essential concept is the payer isn't the same as the receiver of the services. Too, what coverage do we have? If we have group insurance through our employer, then it depends also on the plan our employer selects. Here we see also that things can be far more complex than the initially appear.
[81] Federal Emergency Management Agency
[82] See "Deficits Don't Matter."

The Trump Organization, the board of directors is usually a collection of the stockholders who then elect a chair of the board, and then appoint themselves to various corporate officer positions. Often the chair and the president are the same person. There is nothing wrong with this: a family restaurant may be incorporated and operate just this way. The point is that the family puts someone in charge who essentially runs the show. This individuals then makes the decisions and hires and fires lower management and employees at will.

Different in government, and specifically in federal government, there are constraints. Many positions, such as cabinet officers, are subject to confirmation by the Senate. The Senate can reject a nominee. Or, the President may confer with key members of the Senate in advance to agree on a compromise candidate that everyone will settle for. In some instances, such as Secretary of State, the President can fire the individual at will. Still, a replacement is subject to Senate confirmation.

In some instances, such as the Federal Reserve Board of Governors, who serve 14-year terms, and cannot be fired by the President. The concept is that they will be insulated from day-to-day politics and be able to make the decisions they see fit, without fear or favor from political agendas or changes in administration during their term.

Budgets have to be approved by Congress. There are built-in conflicts between the President and Congress, as while it is clear that the President is the military commander-in-chief, only Congress can declare war. So we can have military conflicts commanded by the President which are not war. Where there aren't explicit provisions, the Constitution says "The executive power shall be vested in a President…" but doesn't say where that power begins and ends.

The President can issue executive orders (inherently, as someone in an executive position can issue orders. In some cases, these are authorized by Congress, but as in the Arms Control Act, the President shall decide which items can be removed from controls under the U.S. Munitions List, but must report to Congress and then wait 30 days before acting.[83] This gives Congress the opportunity to pass legislation forbidding the President from removing a particular item. But that would have to be signed by the President, or, if vetoed by the President, a passage by 2/3 of both the House of Representatives and Senate to override the President. Constitutional checks and balances specifically written to provide brakes on the exercise of power. How different from a family owned and operated corporation!

So the skillsets required to be an effective President are not only different from the business world, but in many ways contradictory to what would are needed for successful business practices at the executive level.

A President with only business experience has a need to make great adjustments in order to be effective, and refrains from making those adjustments only at his peril and

---

[83] 22 USC 2778, which can be examined at https://www.law.cornell.edu/uscode/text/22/chapter-39/subchapter-III free of charge through the courtesy of Cornell University Law School.

that of the country. A President with business experience who has served one term on a local school board will be better oriented.

But was Donald Trump Successful in the First Place?

And so it is time to consider this key point. Was he in fact successful or not? Is this an absolute, or is it a question of "successful compared to whom?"

There are various versions of his wealth.[84] They seem to settle at him beginning with about the organization his father built having a value of about $1 billion (by the early 1970s) and with it having a present (year 2020) value of about $8 billion on the high side. Let's go with both of these figures and we have an increase of 800% from, say 1971 to 2020. That looks impressive at first, an increase of 16.33% per year based on simple percentages (not compounding). But at times during this period, money market rates were higher than that (and at times much lower).

So let's take a look at a specific real estate situation, 1979-present. In 1979, after my father died, my mother and I sold the house in New Jersey for $37,000 and mother moved to Arizona where I already lived. I have the documents to show this. Current value is harder to prove, and I haven't paid for an appraiser to ask the current owner for a walkthrough, but www.zillow.com reports that it is now worth $367,633. So that is a 10.06% increase. The last reported sale on www.zillow.com was January 29, 2019, at

---

[84] An interesting narrative is at https://www.theatlantic.com/politics/archive/2011/04/weve-been-trying-figure-out-how-much-trump-worth-20-years/349875/

$182,175. So that is a big difference for two years. That would be a 20.31% increase. Average the two and we get 15.19%.

This house has changed hands a number of times since 1979, but there are similar houses in the area. So let's say an average person (cab driver, bartender), bought such a house. Based on this math, Donald Trump's increase in wealth from 1971-2020 was somewhere between 6.27% better than the average person and to 14.04 less to an average of 1.15% better than the average person.

We can expand on this to say that, starting at $37,000 and moving forward, we would need 27,027.03 homebuyers to buy a total of $1 billion of property in 1979. (Let's round that to 27,027 for math we'll do a little further along.)

Put it all together and consider reasonable ranges, and we see that Donald Trump as a real estate investor did more or less as well as the average person did over the same period. **And** we have to give Donald Trump the eight extra years to do it (starting 1971 instead of 1979). **And** we have to give him that he learned everything about real estate, as he puts it, from his father from when he was a little boy onward. **AND** we have to give him that after he knew everything about real estate, he went to Fordham and then University of Pennsylvania for a degree in business. focusing on real estate, to learn more than everything there was to know. And all this just to come up to about average!

But wait! Are we working on net or gross figures? Let's take the $1 billion number. Does that mean there was $1 billion of unencumbered real estate (no mortgages or other loans)? Does that mean there was $1 billion of real estate with $ 1 billion of loans against it all (that is a net value of zero)? Or $2 billion of real estate with only $1 billion of encumbrance (a positive net value of $1 billion to the good.) Or $1 billion of real estate with $2 billion of loans against it (a net value of minus $1 billion, or "underwater" status)?

Donald Trump has not made this clear for the starting or ending figures. But let's assume the best: he started with $1 billion of real estate. So either $1 billion unencumbered or $2 billion with $1 billion of encumbrance, or $10 billion with $9 billion of encumbrance, all come out the same way: a net value of $ 1 billion at the starting point.

In all of these case, we figure an 800% increase from $1 billion to $8 billion over 49 years.

Let's assume that both figures are total figures of the value of the real estate, even with encumbrances. This is admittedly an assumption because we are not sure, but it is comparing apples to apples.

But wait again! Now we have introduced mortgages into the equation. When I sold the house in New Jersey, it was unencumbered (mortgage paid off) but our buyer put down

20%. So their down payment on a $37,000 purchase was $7,400 and they had a mortgage of $31,600 (the remaining 80%). Remember our 27,027 homebuyers above? Let's multiply 27,027 by $7,400 and we get $199,999,800,000. Let's round that to $200 million and we see that for a total of $200 million in down payments, our 27,027 homebuyers are controlling $1 billion of property. Let us imagine that these houses haven't changed hands over time, and the 1979 buyers have paid of their mortgage and still own the property.

Suppose we are correct that the figures we are using for Donald Trump are total values of the property. Suppose we make an assumption (again, an assumption) that the properties are unencumbered and have a total value of $ 1 billion. Today his properties have grown to $ 8 billion, unencumbered (although we understand he does have some mortgages). So his real estate values have still grown 800%.

But the homebuyers of 1979 put up $200 million to buy $1 billion of real estate that is today worth $800 billion. This isn't an 800% increase; it is a 4,000% increase. This would mean that the average cab driver and bartender did five times better than Donald Trump in less time.

But wait again! A 30 year mortgage from 1979 would have been paid off in 2009. As of 2020, that means 11 years of no mortgage, and hence no principal or interest payments for the homebuyers. They could have spent some of this money, invested some, perhaps put some in IRA retirement accounts. We would have to add in whatever they saved over 11 years to come up with a true figure. Let's be modest about and say collectively they save $1 billion. Or even more modest, $500 million. That would be $18,500.19 per homebuyer per year over 11 years. That would mean they put away $1,681.82 per year from the savings on the mortgage, which is $140.15, not counting interest. That seems reasonable. So if we figure that in, their collective investments grew from $200 million in 1979 to $8.5 billion in 2020, or 4250% total increase, compared to Donald Trump's 800%. This means the homebuyers, with no particular real estate experience, did 531% better than Donald Trump.

But wait again! The homebuyers would have been working for a living to earn the money to make the mortgage payments. Donald Trump had tenants pay rent to pay off the mortgages for him. This advantage I cannot put a clear number to, but it undoubtedly an advantage Donald Trump had, plus the extra time, learning from his father, and his bachelor's degree in business all helping propel him forward.
All these advantages and he did less than 1/5 as well as the average person. And he considers all this "amazing." Is he amazed when he can do 1/5 as well as average? The conservatives also seem to consider 1/5 as well as average to be very successful, and to be the mark of a person far more intelligent than average.

Yet in the real world, could we expect that the average person with Trump's advantages, would have done 500% better than Donald Trump was able to do?

Of course, as stated, there are estimates and assumptions here, but as Donald Trump will not produce authenticated information, this is the best we can. I look forward to the day when he may reveal the full information and we can analyze totally from facts. But I expect those analyses will not deviate much from the above.

So, if a successful businessperson with only that experience would not be prepared to take on the Presidency, how can the conservatives conclude that an unsuccessful businessperson would be qualified?

A Builder?

Yes, let's consider his claim "I'm a great builder."[85] Suppose I see a piece of property with a house on it and I want to have it torn down to build a different house. It doesn't matter if I want to rent it out, live in it, or try to sell it at a profit immediately after construction.

I contact a wrecking company (we'll call them the "wrecker") to tear down the house, cap off the gas, and take the other necessary steps to make the property safe, and haul away the debris.

I contact an architect to explain the kind of house I want to build, and the architect gives me some preliminary drawings. Well, I like this and that, but I don't like this over here. I would like a three car garage instead of a two car garage and I will sacrifice a large

---

[85] https://www.nydailynews.com/opinion/ny-oped-the-great-crackup-20201010-23jgizzpvjajferyqjzpbbqryu-story.html and other sources.

dining room and take a smaller one in order to have a larger living room. Eventually, the architect comes up with plans I like, and off we go.

I contact a builder to construct the house, and the builder hires masons, plumbers, carpenters, and other skilled trades to build the house. The painters finish one day and the landscapers the next, and there we are! Ready for occupancy!

But did any of these steps make me a wrecker, an architect, a builder, or a mason, plumber, carpenter, painter, or landscaper? No. No matter how much input I provided as to what I wanted done, I am still a real estate investor and not something else. The more I was involved in the planning, the more I can say "I helped design" but I am still not an architect. If I changed my mind on the living room paint when I saw it and arranged for it to be repainted, that does not make me a painter.

QED: "Quod erat demonstrandum" ("what was to be shown, has been demonstrated.")

Social Security and Medicare

Myths:

"Social Security is socialism and so has no place in the U.S. economy."

"Because Social Security is socialism and so it can't work."

"Social Security is bankrupt. It won't be there when I retire."

"The Ryan Plan is the answer for Medicare."

The First Two

A) See "Socialism and Capitalism."

B) But it did work.

"Social Security is bankrupt. It won't be there when I retire."

No, there are projections that in the future Social Security will become unable to keep its benefits at the current level, based on current income and demographics, and that the trust fund will have dissipated.

First, let me reveal when I first heard the myth. It was 1958 when I was 10 years old, and it wasn't addressed to me. We lived in a two-family house with my father's parents, and one day I was home one of my grandfather's friends stopped by for a beer just as my father was coming home from work. My grandfather's friend told my father, "Social Security is a great help to us but it won't be there when you're ready to retire. The money you are paying in is gone forever. It was a terrible idea to begin with." He was a conservative. So he was happy to draw Social Security himself but was adamantly against it at the same time.

And so here I am drawing Social Security even today, 62 years later. The money is there each month.

But let's address the word "retirement." Many people "retire" from a full-time job but continue to work part-time. Some do so because they need the money, some because they like their work and like the money, some because they want to keep busy and like the money. Some people, on the other hand, volunteer for various causes for free to keep busy and contribute to their community. So, "retirement?" It means different things to different people and I will agree that Social Security makes reference to the word on their own website.

But for people who continue working, paid or volunteer, they have decided not to fully retire. On the other hand, if you win millions of dollars in the lottery at 21 and decide never to work another day, Social Security does not drag you out of your house and make you go to work. (You probably will not have enough working calendar quarters at that point to qualify for Social Security, but then, what do you care?)[86]

You can also begin taking Social Security at different ages, a lower monthly payment the earlier you begin, higher if you wait, up to age 70.[87] So let's consider the month you begin receiving Social Security payments as being that, and not necessarily being identical with your retirement.

The Social Security Act was signed into law by President Franklin D. Roosevelt on August 14, 1935. It had passed Congress by a vote of 372-33 (12 not voting) in the House of Representatives, and 77-6 (12 not voting)[88], although a conference committee

---

[86] As winning the lottery is not a secure retirement plan, and retirement savings and for some of us, pensions are important, so is Social Security. Checking your account to see how many quarters you have, what the rules are for eventually qualifying for benefits, and then estimating your benefits, is important personal financial planning, and you don't need to hire a financial planner to do it. See www.ssa.gov for plenty of information.

[87] Under current law, the last increase comes when you celebrate your 70th birthday. So if you wait until after that, you receive no more increases, you are just giving up the payments you are entitled so. I recommend filing a few months before the month you want to begin receiving payments.

[88] https://www.ssa.gov/history/1930.html

was called to work out some details prior to final passage. So initially it was very popular among most Democrats and Republicans (although the Democrats did have a large majority in each house).[89] The first cards were issued in 1937, and the first monthly benefit check issued in 1940. It grew over time as it originally did not cover all working people, or include spousal benefits.

What has most changed the Social Security financial situation over all this time? Clearly, people are living longer. Much longer. Oversimplified, but they are paying in for the same number of years and drawing out for much longer. Because the senior population lives so long, its percentage of the population has increased. In 1940, we had a ratio of 159.4 covered workers (paying in) for each retiree, and in 2018, we had 2.8 covered workers for each retiree. As stated above, though, we do have some members of our population working and drawing benefits at the same time. So we do have to keep that in the backs of our minds. Still, the ratio has changed enormously.

The Trust Fund

It is true that the money in the Social Security trust fund is diminishing. But that doesn't mean Social Security is insolvent. Some say, "there is no money in the Social Security trust fund." Of course not. We don't want money in the trust fund. Suppose I set up a trust fund for a teenage relative for $1,000,000 (**he** should live so long!). I put the money into the account this morning. Since I am not satisfied with the low return of bank interest, I invest the money in various stocks and bonds to the tune of $1,000,000 by

---

[89] But as the 74th Congress convened, there were 322 Democrats and 102 Republicans in the House of Representatives, and there were 68 Democrats and 25 Republicans in the Senate. So clearly, with Democrats in the majority in all committees, their ideas about Social Security prevailed.

5:00 P.M. Now how much money is in the trust fund? Zero! But that doesn't mean that the trust fund has a **value** of zero. It has a value of $1,000,000 which I hope will grow nicely over time.

So there is no money in the Social Security trust fund either. What is there instead? U.S. government bonds. Some Republicans say, "there is no money in the Social Security trust fund because Congress has already spent all that money." No, there is no money in the Social Security trust fund because Congress has spent money, the Treasury has issued bonds (borrowed) to pay for the excess spending (budget deficit) and various entities have bought the bonds. China has bought some.[90] Canada, too. U.S. banks, also. If you have an IRA or 401(k) or 403(b)[91] mutual fund, it likely holds some U.S. bonds. It may also hold some city, county, or state bonds, and/or some foreign bonds. Or some corporate bonds. There are lots of bonds.

So is the government borrowing from itself? No, the Social Security trust fund has used some money to purchase some U.S. government bonds just like all the others can. Because it is a trust fund, it is an entity distinct from U.S. government funds. If I decide to buy U.S. government bonds for my teenager's trust fund, then the trust fund exchanges money for the bonds, collects the interest, and eventually can present the bond for repayment of the principal (original amount paid for the bond). Just like anyone else. But it is **not** my money and the government hasn't spent the money in my trust

---

[90] See "China and Tariffs"

[91] The 403(b) is the equivalent of a 401(k) generally for nonprofit organizations; many teachers at community colleges, for example, can contribute to a 403(b) but not a 401(k). These are just references to the location of the provisions in the Tax Code.

fund either. It has spent money that it has borrowed and I happen to have arranged for my trust fund to buy some of that debt.

This can seem complicated, but keep relating it to my teenager's trust fund and it will make sense. The Social Security trust fund (liabilities of the U.S. government, but assets of the trust fund) is close to $3,000,000,000,000 ($3 trillion).[92]

Why does the Social Security Administration invest in U.S. government bonds? Well, what are the other choices?

#1 We can have only cash (currency) in the trust fund but then there won't be enough currency to fill the petty cash needs of the economy.[93] Plus, where would we store it all?

#2 We can invest in stocks, but then a trust fund that is administered by a U.S. government institution will decide which stocks to buy and sell and when, and with $3,000,000,000,000 to invest, it can rock the market on a daily basis with the decisions it makes. Plus, it's more socialism (government ownership of the means of production and/or distribution).[94]

---

[92] For those who want to examine the matter in detail, good information is available at
https://www.ssa.gov/policy/docs/statcomps/supplement/2019/4a.html ;
https://www.ssa.gov/history/tftable.html has historical information in a simpler form but updating was discontinued with the 2009 data. https://www.treasurydirect.gov/govt/reports/pd/feddebt/feddebt_daily.htm can also be of interest.
[93] See "Creating Money, The Budget, The Deficit, and The Debt"
[94] See "Socialism and Capitalism"

#3 We can invest in foreign stocks and bonds, but then we are helping foreign companies and governments with capital that could have stayed here.

So purchasing U.S. government bonds, which have a total issuance of some seven times what the Social Security Administration holds (therefore the Social Security Administration's activities buying and selling[95] U.S. government bonds on any given day are not significant enough to rock the bond market) seems like the best option.

And so there we are. But where are we? Why do we need a trust fund in the first place and why is it diminishing?

Answer #1: Me. And other baby boomers. Because of the ratio, the amount of money being paid in is not sufficient to cover what is being drawn out. Information at the websites shown in footnote 7 bear this out. So this is a savings account built up over time so that the assets (U.S. government bonds) can be redeemed or sold according to the need for money to pay beneficiaries. Accountants will refer to this as cash flow management.

Answer #2: The Republican Party. We need the reserve funds to be available for when the Republicans are in power and apply their fiscal conservative policies which cause recessions.[96] At these times, unemployment increases and people out of work don't pay

---

[95] The Social Security Trust Fund can buy bonds when issued by the Treasury, or on the open market from someone else (perhaps your mutual fund) who owns some bonds and is ready to sell to raise cash. It can hold bonds until maturity and then redeem them or it can sell bonds on the open market, just like your mutual fund or anyone else, depending on when the money is needed. Then there is money in the trust fund, short-term, as it is quickly on its way out to beneficiaries..

[96] Some exceptions, but see https://www.cnbc.com/2020/04/09/what-happened-in-every-us-recession-since-the-great-depression.html

into Social Security but the outflow remains high, and always growing as our senior population increases. So the savings account, or trust fund, helps take care of ensuring that the payments are made during these rough times.

Abortion

Myths:

"Elect us. We are going to overturn *Roe v. Wade* and stop abortions."

"The Republican Party is opposed to abortions."

Background

As an overview we have the three branches. So *Roe v. Wade, a Supreme Court decision,* is the principal factor preventing state governments (or the federal governments) from making most abortions illegal. It was decided on privacy grounds, and we do have a tradition and various legislation (e.g., HIPPA) of privacy between the patient and the medical provider.

Where do we find a right to privacy in the Constitution? The Fourth Amendment provides a right in terms of search and seizure; the First Amendment would permit us to pray privately without having to let anyone know about it. If we would consider writing a letter to the editor on an issue, we can draft it in private, and then even throw the draft away, and never send it. So there is something of an implied right to privacy, but not very strong or clear.

Roe v. Wade relied heavily on the provisions of the Ninth Amendment. But there was an argument based on the Tenth Amendment that states did have the power to make abortion illegal.

An important point regarding *Roe v. Wade:* There are groups advertising (and asking for your money) that say, "we need your help to overturn *Roe v. Wade* because then abortions will stop." Sometimes it is "**We are going to overturn *Roe v. Wade* and make abortions illegal.**" Various conservative groups use these approaches, and certainly the Republican Party. But let's take a close look.

First, overturning *Roe v. Wade would not make abortions illegal. It* would allow states to legislate abortion as a crime (illegal). But once a state does so, then women seeking an abortion can go a neighboring state for an abortion, or get an illegal one in their own state.

The Supreme Court is an issue at election time only for certain Americans. It boils down to many people in what is called the Pro-Life movement voting for Republicans, donating money, and putting up signs. There are Americans who vote solely on one issue, and many of them focus exclusively on abortion. Others, who appear to be fewer, on the Pro-Choice side, support Democratic candidates.

Even if the Supreme Court Justices were all 100% in favor of overturning *Roe v. Wade,* and believe they see legal grounds for doing so, they cannot reach out to overturn it. Of the three branches of government, this is the one branch that cannot see a situation and take its own action. They have to wait for a case to be appealed to it. This means that there has to be a law against abortion that someone breaks, and the case is successfully appealed all the way up. There are a few cases floating around.[97] How many years this would take, **if** it was successful, is an open question.

So then it is in the hands of the state legislatures, and possibly Congress would consider a national law forbidding abortions. Let's focus on the state legislatures.

Suppose we are in a state with 30 members of the state senate. We'll also have the state Assembly and the governor, but for the moment we have a bill before the state senate. Those who want to outlaw abortion need 16 votes (majority) to pass the bill and send it to the state assembly.

Based on the polls[98], let's say we have almost a 50/50 split between those in favor of outlawing abortion and those opposed, but let's give one side a clear edge. We have 20

---

[97] A pending case in the lower courts is discussed here: https://www.usnews.com/news/us/articles/2020-08-12/georgia-appeals-ruling-that-blocked-restrictive-abortion-law
[98] See next section. "The Enforcement Dilemma."

votes in favor of outlawing abortion and only 10 opposed. At first glance, it looks like this is a bill that will easily sail right through.

But the 20 in favor are not really one faction. They are in four factions of five each.

Faction A: Outlaw all abortions.

Faction B: Outlaw all abortions except those resulting from rape.

Faction C: Outlaw all abortions except those resulting from incest.

Faction D: Outlaw all abortions except those resulting from rape or incest.

So here we end up with four different factions which absolutely disagree about what the bill should say. We end up with five votes in favor, the 10 solidly against, and then the 15 opposed because it is not what they believe is the correct policy. Bill fails soundly. There is no room for the four actions to negotiate a compromise among themselves on the text of a final bill because there is no room for them to compromise between those positions. You are either in one faction or another and you could only "move to" another faction, which other members of your faction will see you as selling out.

Now consider the state assembly, and whether the governor is in favor of the final bill, or is against it altogether, and multiply it by 50 states plus the District of Columbia. We are a long way from any concept that if *Roe v. Wade* is overturned, abortions stop tomorrow.

We can pause here to ask if the Republicans are really in favor of antiabortion bills, or if that is a Conservative Republican myth. Remember there are large numbers of single-issue voters who are consistently voting Republican because "next year they will end abortions once and for all!" (The Republicans have been selling that idea since 1974.) These voters also donate money, put bumper stickers on their cars, and yard signs in front of their houses. That's a lot of support. But if they ever made abortion illegal, then these voters will be satisfied. Then they will find another issue. Perhaps it is an issue where 50% of them side with the Republicans and 50% with the Democrats. Now by doing what your constituency wanted you to do, you have lost 50% of them (potentially). Why not keep making promises year after year, decade after decade, with a strategy of convincing enough people that you are right on the verge of getting it done, but never actually do it, and keep them under your control? Well, there is an ethical "why not" but that doesn't seem to matter to the Conservative Republicans. They are getting the support they want, and that is what counts to them.

The Enforcement Dilemma

If, as the years would go by, abortion would become illegal in every state (not guaranteed because there is strong opposition Polls on Abortion), then we would still have abortions; they would just be illegal.

Many people do not grasp that because something is illegal does not mean it is impossible to do it. Bank robberies, overtime parking, and littering are all legal, but it is possible to commit these offenses. Before *Roe v. Wade,* there were lots of abortions (I have a cousin who had an abortion); they were just illegal. To stop abortions would then require increased policing and enforcement. So we would need an action plan, organization chart, flow chart, budget for additional police, courts and prisons, and then decide whose taxes are going up, in order to actually deal with the crime.

But if the state successfully prosecutes those who performed/ received an abortion, and sends them to prison, that still didn't stop the abortion. The conviction would be based on the prosecutor proving to a jury that an abortion occurred. So the idea that all this would stop abortions is somewhat flawed. Enforcement is based on abortions being successful.

How might we empower the police to stop abortions and make the arrests for an *attempted* abortion? There is a very short window. An abortion is about to be attempted.

The police enter in force to make an arrest and the woman says, "Oh, is this an abortion center? I just came in to ask for directions to the junkyard." The would-be abortionist says, "I collect medical equipment like some people collect stamps." Neither is doing anything illegal.

But come in too late, and the abortion is complete, even though the procedure is not complete. That is, the fetus is dead. So now we are back to where we were. Police will have a brief window of opportunity to come in between the time they are prepared to begin the procedure, and the time the abortion is complete. And how long will it take to get a search warrant? Or will there be searches without warrants, which then bring in Fourth Amendment issues.

How will this all work? The Conservative Republicans will not tell. Most have not thought it through. Most are simply misconnecting the dots from *Roe v. Wade* to illegal to a zero level of abortions. Some perhaps really believe what they are saying. Some perhaps understand they are misdirecting people in order to keep them supporting Republicans.

So this is more complicated than some of the advocates of the cause admit, or in some cases understand. The emphasis of many who say they want to stop abortions, is really to make sure they are illegal when they happen, not to stop them.

Some conservatives are not opposed to states outlawing abortion, but noting that, as discussed, if abortion is illegal in New Jersey, someone could go across the border to New York or Pennsylvania as long as it is still legal there. The conservatives conclude, then, that the decision that abortions should be illegal must be made at a national level, applying to all Americans in every state and territory. (Still, that doesn't necessarily stop any abortions, that just means when abortions are done, they will be illegal, as prior to *Roe v. Wade*. The conservatives generally are not talking about increased police surveillance dedicated to finding abortion clinics or women thinking of having abortions, or about funding for additional courtrooms and prisons, or other measures that would be related to enforcement of the law.)

In the end, if we step away from Conservative Republicans and consider the Pro-Life groups generally, we find many people who are very sincerely opposed to abortion (from the point of view of one of the four factions). There are opportunities for them to try to stop abortions, such as helping alternative birthing centers, support for unwed mothers, and others, and many of them go out of their way to help. But when they support the Republican Party, they cease helping to stop abortions and start helping a party whose vested interest is in keeping abortions legal and pretending they are opposed to legal abortions at the same time.

Cause and Effect: Illegal Abortions and then what?

But suppose the Pro-Life groups do successfully make abortions illegal. The enforcement is a difficult matter. So the end result can well be that we have the same number of abortions; they are just illegal. So the medical doctor down the road does abortions after hours for $1,000 cash, the veterinarian does them after hours for $500 cash, and some character does abortions in his garage with kitchen tools for $50 cash. This is what was going on before. So we still have the abortions, but in the latter case, we have more women being injured and sometimes dying in the process as a result of the unsanitary conditions and sloppy procedures. So if the Pro-Life groups as such as in favor of illegal abortions, should they really call themselves the Pro-Death groups, as being in favor of continuing abortions but then add the deaths of more women as a result?

The argument sometimes come up, "with all these arguments about making abortions illegal being the wrong way to go, you might as well advocate legalizing bank robbery." But not the same thing.

Sometimes we have bank robberies in the dead of night, and sometimes while the bank is open. A break-in can trigger a silent alarm, a daylight robbery can result in bank personnel triggering a silent alarm. I am thinking of the kinds of alarms that don't make a sound on-site, but go off at a central dispatch who calls the police. So it could be stopped in-progress as an **attempted** robbery. Too, a passerby might notice what is going on and make a 911 call.

If the robbery is successful, still, we have video camera footage and we may have witnesses day or night. Perhaps someone used a phone to take a picture of the getaway car including the license plate. Perhaps someone even has a phone video of the whole thing! Great evidence! And the witness can call the police directly and we can prosecute on a **successful** robbery.

What should we not expect? We should not expect the bank robber or any accomplice (such as a bank employee or customer) to make the police call, or record the video, or take any other steps that can help the prosecution.

So, trying to make the analogy from the crime of bank robbery to a crime of attempted or successful abortion doesn't work. Who will be taking these actions? Can we expect either the abortionist or the woman seeking the abortion to call 911 and say, "yes, we're about to perform an abortion here. Send a car right over to stop us before we're successful and arrest us." Or, "we just performed a successful abortion and now we want to be arrested and prosecuted. We'll stand by and wait for you."

No, both have a goal of a successful abortion and not being arrested or prosecuted. Can we add in others, such as an abortionist's assistance and the boyfriend who is paying for the abortion? Would any of them want to make the call? And they wouldn't normally be recording a video that could be used in evidence. What about a witness passing by? An illegal abortion clinic is not going to have the big windows of a bank lobby providing visibility, and much less so if it is an amateur in his garage.

Where Does This Leave Us?

I will say simply that I have met many liberals who are opposed to abortions and also opposed to Big Government making abortions illegal. They are also opposed to people who pretend to be against abortion because of their own hidden agenda. Instead, they join with many other antiabortion individuals who contribute to the alternate birthing centers, support for unwed mothers, as mentioned above, and other causes. These are ways of stopping more abortions than any effort to make them illegal ever would (and that is making them illegal was a viable plan in the first place).

Know what else? I have never met anyone is truly anti-abortion. I have talked with many women over the years, including Roman Catholics and Church of Jesus Christ of Latter Day Saints (Mormons), whose religions preach vigorously against abortions, who say, "I would never have an abortion, but I don't want Big Government telling anyone they should or shouldn't have one." I have talked with women who have had an abortion, and individuals where the abortion was another family member, and heard stories about extenuating circumstances of one sort or another and great anguish that we don't need to get into here. These were not decisions made easily and were under extreme stress. No one involved was every happy about it. Know what, though? I have never met anyone in the United States who takes a position that I could truly call "Pro-Abortion." I have also never met a Conservative Republican who can prove there is such a person. But that doesn't prevent them throwing the term around in name-calling of people who are truly Right to Choose.

Here is an article quoting Pastor Robert Jefrress, a television preacher: (https://www.newsweek.com/trumps-evangelical-allies-defensive-after-pastor-suggests-presidents-arrogance-deadlier-1544247).

Weathervanes

If we have a philosophy, a firm belief, a definite point of view, then we should be apply the same rules to different situations. The Conservative Republicans spin like weathervanes, depending on the situation. Here, we'll look at the situation first and the myth second.

Weathervane Set #1

Point of View #1

1989-1993 George W. Bush is a Republican President with a Democratic Congress (both houses) all four years.

Myth: "Well, see, if the Democrats were good Americans and understood how things are supposed to be, they would accept that the President and the Vice-President are the only officials elected by the entire country. Of the two, the President is the one with the power. Therefore, the Democrats should accept that the country wants a Republican President to make decisions the Republican way and just set their ideas aside and approve whatever the President sends over to Congress. If the public likes what the Republicans do, they can vote the Republicans back in. If they don't, they can vote the Democrats in. That's the American way."

Point of View #2

1993-1995 Bill Clinton is a Democratic President with a Democratic Congress for these two years.

Myth: "Well, see, if the Democrats were good Americans and understood how things are supposed to be, they would accept that the Republicans, while in the minority in both houses, still won election district-by-district and state-by-state and their voters should not be disenfranchised. Therefore, the Democrats should show bipartisanship and set their ideas aside and approve the Republican ideas."

Point of View #3

1997-2001 Bill Clinton is a Democratic President with a Republican Congress for these two years.

Myth: "Well, see, if the Democrats were good Americans and understood how things are supposed to be, they would accept that Congress, elected district-by-district and state-by-state, is always closer to the will of the people than the President. Therefore, the

Republicans, having the majority in both houses, should be setting policy, passing what they see fit, and the Democratic President should just sign whatever they send over.

Point of View #4

2001-2007 George W. Bush is a Republican President with a mostly Republican Congress for these six years.[99]

Myth: "Well, see, if the Democrats were good Americans and understood how things are supposed to be, they would accept that the Republicans have the Presidency and both House of Congress. So it is clear that the people want the Republicans to set the policies. Therefore, the Democrats should sit quietly and let the Republican President and the Republican Congress run the country."

Point of View #5

2008-2009 George W. Bush is a Republican President with a Democratic Congress for these two years.

Repeat #1.

Point of View #6

2009-2013 Barack Obama is a Democratic President with a Democratic Congress for his first two years, and with a Democratic House and Republican Senate 2011-2013.

Repeat #4.

---

[99] A Republican Congress in both houses, except for 2001-2003 with a Republican House and a Democratic Senate. So this situation becomes a little more complex during those two years. We'll keep the example simple.

Point of View #7

2008-2009 George W. Bush is a Republican President with a Democratic Congress for these two years.

Repeat #1.

And so it goes. The Republicans spin around like a weathervane, with no true belief of their own other than: "no matter how the election turns out, everything should always go our way. That's only fair."

I can accept anyone having any one of these points of view. But I can't accept the same people spinning around to different, opposing points of view on a continuing basis.

Weathervane Set #2

Point of View #1

"Bill Clinton is a terrible President because he is a womanizer. He doesn't have the moral character to be President. He should resign."

Point of View #2

"Donald Trump is a womanizer, but we all have our faults. A person doesn't have to be of good moral character to be President. All of us are imperfect and should be forgiving of Donald Trump's imperfections."

Weathervane Set #3

Point of View #1

"Donald Trump has the authority to do X, Y, and Z, and so he's doing. So shut up. As long as he has the authority, you have no right to criticize."

Point of View #1

"Barack Obama may have the authority to do X, Y, and Z, but he isn't doing the right thing, so we are free to criticize. Just because he has the authority doesn't mean he's right."

Weathervane Set #3

Point of View #1

"Donald Trump is President of the United States. You should show respect for him because of the office he holds."

Point of View #2

"Bill Clinton is President of the United States and deserves only our contempt, President or not."

Weathervane Set #4

Point of View #1

"Bill Clinton is just a terrible President. He's not getting anything done" (spoken January 2, 1993, 18 days before Bill Clinton took office).

Point of View #2

"Come on, now. You have to give Reagan/Bush/Trump a chance. He's only been office a week/a month/a year" (A consistent point of view whenever a Republican takes office and throughout his administration.).

Weathervane Set #5

Point of View #1

"President Bush is the President of the United States, doing what he thinks is best for the country. If you don't like the way the country is run, you should just get out of the country."

Point of View #2

"President Obama is the President of the United States and…(criticism, criticism, criticism)." But I did not see one Conservative Republican, true to what they **said** their values were, pack their bags and get out of the country.

No Matter What

No matter what, the weathervanes spin.

A Democratic President is in office and is criticized, even condemned, for X, Y, and Z. "He's terrible," beginning from Day One.

A Republican President is in office and the Conservative Republicans unite in saying, "now let's not point the finger." "Let's give him a chance." Day after day, month after month, year after year, he still needs a chance.

Sometimes we have a Republican President and a Democratic House of Representatives and Senate, and the Republicans whine, "I don't understand why the Democrats don't just pass whatever the President wants. That's what Congress is for." But that is not what the Constitution says, and that is not what the Republicans say when the situation is reversed.

And so spin the weathervanes.

Afterword

So here we complete pages and pages of discussion and I hope it has been informative for you.

Here I ask this of you: find a book on conservative politics and policy, or a conservative to talk to, and get that point of you. I don't, of course, mean someone who is screaming, "Zodl wants to live under a socialist dictatorship. I don't want any socialism anywhere in America…." and so on. I mean someone who can provide you with facts and logic, as I have tried to do, and present a clear and reasonable case for the conservative side.

Then, as it should be, it is up to you to make up your own mind.

END